MICROWAVE COOKING TIMES
AT A GLANCE!

An A-Z

MICROWAVE COOKING TIMES AT A GLANCE!

AN A-Z

Annette Yates

RIGHT WAY

Constable & Robinson Ltd
3 The Lanchesters
162 Fulham Palace Road
London W6 9ER
www.constablerobinson.com

First published in the UK 1997.
This edition published by Right Way,
an imprint of Constable & Robinson, 2011

A copy of the British Library Cataloguing in
Publication Data is available from the British Library

ISBN: 978-0-7160-2067-7

Printed and bound in the EU

1 3 5 7 9 10 8 6 4 2

ABOUT THE AUTHOR

Annette Yates is a home economist who has enjoyed using, and writing about, microwaves ever since the first domestic models were put on sale in the UK.

Annette was born in South Wales and grew up in the Brecon Beacons. Since training as a home economist in London, she has worked on educational magazines, school's presentations and a consumer help-line for a major food manufacturer. She has written many features on microwaves for consumer magazines and has organised demonstrations at large food exhibitions, as well as running her own microwave cookery classes. Annette also enjoys styling food for photography.

Whatever her current project, she is usually to be found creating recipes in her own kitchen – her family and friends being her best critics. Annette is author of several cookery books and is a member of the Microwave Association and of the Guild of Food Writers. She currently lives in South Wales with her husband and two student daughters.

Illustrations by
Lindsay Thomas

AUTHOR'S NOTES

This is a book of microwave cooking times – a handy reference to keep within arm's reach of your microwave.

Your manufacturer's handbook and cookbook should of course be your first points of reference (after all, their cooking times have been tested in your model). However, there may be occasions when a food is not listed and you don't feel confident about putting it in the microwave. On occasions like these, simply look up the food here.

Whatever the wattage of your microwave, each entry in this book tells you the best power level to use, together with an approximate cooking time. I say 'approximate' because microwave cookers, like conventional cookers, can vary in their performance. Two cookers from two different manufacturers are likely to behave slightly differently, even though the wattage is the same in both.

The charts in this book are based on a range of power levels which will be easy to match up with the settings on your own microwave. They are:

HIGH (100%)
MED-HIGH (70-80%)
MEDIUM (50%)
MED-LOW (30%) and
LOW (10%).

DEFROST settings are usually equivalent to MED-LOW (30%).

On most occasions it is fine to cook on HIGH (100%) but there are foods that cook better on lower power levels. Each chart lists the best power level to use in your cooker. Those of you with high-wattage microwaves will notice that

I suggest cooking some foods and, in particular, small quantities, on MED-HIGH, MEDIUM or even lower. This is because HIGH can often be too fierce, causing the food to spit, burn or dry up around its edges. It is also worth remembering:

- If you find that foods cook too fast in your microwave, don't hesitate to turn the power level down slightly. It may take a little longer to cook (by a few seconds or a minute or two) but the result will be worth it. Resist the temptation to stick rigidly to the power levels and cooking times given in a book if you get better results by adjusting them slightly. Like conventional cookers, you have to get the 'feel' of your microwave in order to cook with confidence.

- If you have been cooking certain foods successfully on HIGH until now, stay with it! You may also have found that some foods benefit from cooking on a lower power. Be encouraged by this – it means that you are already getting the 'feel' of your microwave cooker.

- In the charts, some times given for high-wattage cookers may *seem* long compared to others – this is due to the low power level which, in my testing, usually produces better results. Remember, faster is not always best! Try out the power level and time given in the chart first; then, if you think the food could tolerate a slightly higher power level, next time try it. You will soon know exactly how to get the best results in *your* microwave.

- Always test dishes in the conventional way to check that the food is cooked to your liking. Are the vegetables soft enough? Is the chicken cooked through? Is the meat tender? Has the sauce thickened? Is it bubbling around the edges? Is it piping hot throughout? These are just some of the questions that should come to mind – just as they would when you are cooking conventionally.

At the risk of sounding boring, I must urge you to check the cooking instructions on food packs. Food manufacturers go to great pains to include microwave methods if they are appropriate, and usually give at least two cooking times (on two different wattages) on their packs. Don't worry if the wattage of your cooker is not listed. You have two alternatives, both of which are simple. You can work out (from the two that are listed on the pack) an approximate cooking time, and then check to see if the food is cooked. Alternatively, you can use a power level which is equivalent to one of the wattages listed on the food pack, and cook for the given time.

You will notice that this book lists *foods* and not specific *recipes*. A huge selection of recipes is to be found in my other titles which are listed on page 2.

Finally, I would like to thank the microwave manufacturers (and Sharp Electronics in particular for their most recent help) for the loan of microwave cookers over several years. Without their continued assistance I would not have been able to cook so many foods in so many different microwaves!

Annette Yates

A

Aduki Beans

See Pulses.

Apple Sauce

See Apples: Purée.

Apples

Baked

Core each apple and fill with mincemeat, marzipan or a mixture of brown sugar, butter and mixed spice. Using a sharp knife, cut into the skin around the middle of each apple to prevent it bursting. Arrange in a circle in a dish. Cook uncovered until just tender throughout. Leave to stand for a few minutes before serving.

APPLES – whole	500W	600-700W	750-850W	900-1000W
1 medium	HIGH 3-4 min	HIGH 2-3 min	MED-HIGH 2-3 min	MEDIUM 3-4 min
2 medium	HIGH 4-6 min	HIGH 3-5 min	MED-HIGH 3-5 min	MEDIUM 4-6 min
4 medium	HIGH 6-9 min	HIGH 5-7 min	HIGH 4-6 min	MED-HIGH 4-6 min

Slices or Purée

Peel, core and thinly slice fresh apples. Put frozen or fresh apple slices into a casserole (no need to add extra liquid unless you want to), cover and cook until soft or puréed, stirring occasionally. To make apple sauce, stir sugar and butter to taste into the hot purée.

APPLES – sliced	500W	600-700W	750-850W	900-1000W
115g/4 oz	HIGH 2-3 min	HIGH 1$\frac{1}{2}$ to 2$\frac{1}{2}$ min	MED-HIGH 1$\frac{1}{2}$ to 2$\frac{1}{2}$ min	MEDIUM 2-3 min
225g/8 oz	HIGH 5-7 min	HIGH 4-6 min	HIGH 3-5 min	MED-HIGH 3-5 min
450g/1 lb	HIGH 7-9 min	HIGH 6-8 min	HIGH 5-7 min	HIGH 4-6 min

Reheating

Put cooked apple slices or purée into a covered dish. In all models, simply cook on MEDIUM, stirring occasionally, until hot throughout.

Apricots

Halve and stone the apricots. Put into a casserole (no need to add extra liquid unless you want to), cover and cook until soft, stirring gently occasionally. Sweeten to taste.

APRICOTS	500W	600-700W	750-850W	900-1000W
115g/4 oz	HIGH 3-4 min	HIGH 2-3 min	MED-HIGH 2-3 min	MEDIUM 3-4 min
225g/8 oz	HIGH 5-7 min	HIGH 4-6 min	HIGH 3-5 min	MED-HIGH 3-5 min
450g/1 lb	HIGH 7-9 min	HIGH 6-8 min	HIGH 5-7 min	HIGH 4-6 min

Artichokes

Globe Artichokes

Arrange the artichokes upright in a casserole and add 2-4 tbsp water. Cover and cook until tender, rearranging them once or twice.

GLOBE ARTICHOKES	500W	600-700W	750-850W	900-1000W
1	HIGH 6-7 min	HIGH 5-6 min	MED-HIGH 5-6 min	MED-HIGH 4-5 min
2	HIGH 9-10 min	HIGH 7-8 min	MED-HIGH 7-8 min	MED-HIGH 6-7 min
3	HIGH 14-15 min	HIGH 11-12 min	MED-HIGH 11-12 min	MED-HIGH 8-9 min
4	HIGH 16-17 min	HIGH 12-13 min	HIGH 10-11 min	MED-HIGH 10-11 min

Reheating

Cooked globe artichokes are not really suitable for reheating. Canned artichoke hearts can be heated (in all models), covered, on MEDIUM until hot throughout, stirring occasionally.

Jerusalem Artichokes

Scrub or peel the artichokes and halve or slice them. Put into a casserole and add 2-4 tbsp water. Cover and cook until just tender, stirring once or twice.

JERUSALEM ARTICHOKES	500W	600-700W	750-850W	900-1000W
115g/4 oz	HIGH 4-5 min	HIGH 3-4 min	MED-HIGH 3-4 min	MED-HIGH 2-3 min
225g/8 oz	HIGH 7-8 min	HIGH 5-6 min	HIGH 4-5 min	MED-HIGH 4-5 min
450g/1 lb	HIGH 9-10 min	HIGH 7-8 min	HIGH 6-7 min	MED-HIGH 6-7 min

Reheating

Cooked Jerusalem artichokes are best reheated in a sauce. In all models, simply cover and cook on MEDIUM until hot throughout, stirring occasionally.

Asparagus

Frozen

Tip the frozen asparagus into a casserole, cover and cook until just tender, gently separating and rearranging the stalks once or twice.

ASPARAGUS	500W	600-700W	750-850W	900-1000W
115g/4 oz	HIGH 5-6 min	HIGH 4-5 min	MED-HIGH 4-5 min	MED-HIGH 3-4 min
225g/8 oz	HIGH 8-9 min	HIGH 6-7 min	HIGH 5-6 min	MED-HIGH 5-6 min
450g/1 lb	HIGH 10-12 min	HIGH 8-9 min	HIGH 6-7 min	MED-HIGH 6-7 min

Fresh

Arrange the asparagus in an even layer in a dish. Add 2-4 tbsp water. Cover and cook until just tender, gently rearranging the stalks occasionally.

ASPARAGUS	500W	600-700W	750-850W	900-1000W
115g/4 oz	HIGH 4-5 min	HIGH 3-4 min	MED-HIGH 3-4 min	MED-HIGH 3-4 min
225g/8 oz	HIGH 7-8 min	HIGH 5-6 min	HIGH 3-4 min	MED-HIGH 3-4 min
450g/1 lb	HIGH 9-12 min	HIGH 7-9 min	HIGH 4-6 min	MED-HIGH 4-6 min

Reheating

Cooked asparagus is not really suitable for reheating. Canned asparagus should be heated (in all models), covered, on MEDIUM, until hot throughout, stirring gently occasionally.

Aubergines

Slice the aubergines or cut them into bite-size cubes. Put them into a casserole with 2-4 tbsp water, cover and cook until just tender, stirring occasionally.

AUBERGINES	500W	600-700W	750-850W	900-1000W
115g/4 oz	HIGH 3-4 min	HIGH 2-3 min	MED-HIGH 2-3 min	MED-HIGH 2-3 min
225g/8 oz	HIGH 4-5 min	HIGH 3-4 min	HIGH 3-4 min	MED-HIGH 3-4 min
450g/1 lb	HIGH 6-8 min	HIGH 5-6 min	HIGH 4-5 min	HIGH 4-5 min

Reheating
Cooked aubergines are best reheated in a sauce. In all models, simply cover and cook on MEDIUM until hot throughout, stirring occasionally.

Baby Foods

Empty the food into a small serving bowl. Stir well once or twice during heating. Before serving, it is important to stir the food again and to test the temperature carefully – to check that it is not too hot.

BABY FOODS	500W	600-700W	750-850W	900-1000W
128g jar/can	HIGH 40 sec	HIGH 30 sec	MED-HIGH 30 sec	MEDIUM 40 sec

Baby Milk

Stir or shake the milk well and pour into a sterilised wide-neck bottle (do not fit the teat until after heating). Before serving, it is important to shake the milk well and to test the temperature carefully (to make sure that it is not too hot).

BABY MILK	500W	600-700W	750-850W	900-1000W
125ml/4 fl oz	HIGH 40-50 sec	HIGH 20-30 sec	MED-HIGH 20-30 sec	MEDIUM 40-50 sec
225ml/8 fl oz	HIGH 50-60 sec	HIGH 40-50 sec	MED-HIGH 40-50 sec	MEDIUM 50-60 sec

Bacon

Thawing

Remove any metal ties. Stand the meat on a rack in a shallow dish. Cover and microwave, turning over (joints) or separating (chops and rashers) occasionally and pouring away any moisture which collects beneath the rack. Take care not to overheat the bacon, otherwise some areas will begin to cook while other parts are still frozen. Leave joints to stand at least 30 min before cooking, chops and rashers for 10 min.

BACON – thawing	500W	600-700W	750-850W	900-1000W
joints: **per 450g/1 lb**	DEFROST 9-10 min	DEFROST 7-8 min	DEFROST 6-7 min	LOW 7-10 min
chops/rashers/ gammon: **115g/4 oz**	DEFROST 6-8 min	DEFROST 4-6 min	DEFROST 3-5 min	LOW 4-6 min
225g/8 oz	DEFROST 8-9 min	DEFROST 6-7 min	DEFROST 5-6 min	LOW 6-8 min
per 450g/1 lb	DEFROST 10-12 min	DEFROST 8-10 min	DEFROST 7-9 min	LOW 7-9 min
cubes: **115g/4 oz**	DEFROST 4-6 min	DEFROST 3-5 min	DEFROST 3-4 min	LOW 4-6 min
225g/8 oz	DEFROST 6-8 min	DEFROST 5-7 min	DEFROST 4-6 min	LOW 6-8 min
per 450g/1 lb	DEFROST 9-12 min	DEFROST 7-10 min	DEFROST 6-8 min	LOW 7-9 min

Cooking

Joints – put on a rack in a shallow dish and cover with a split microwave or roasting bag. Turn over occasionally during cooking.

Chops and gammon are best cooked on a preheated browning dish – follow the manufacturer's instructions and turn the chops over once during cooking.

Rashers – arrange on a roasting rack with a plate beneath it to catch the drips. A sheet of kitchen paper, laid over the top, absorbs the splashes – to prevent the paper sticking, remove it as soon as the bacon is sufficiently cooked.

BACON	500W	600-700W	750-850W	900-1000W
joints: per 450g/1 lb	HIGH 12-15 min	HIGH 9-12 min	MED-HIGH 9-12 min	MEDIUM 12-15 min
rashers: 2	HIGH 3-4 min	HIGH 2-3 min	MED-HIGH 2-3 min	MED-HIGH 1½ to 2½ min
4	HIGH 5-6 min	HIGH 4-5 min	MED-HIGH 4-5 min	MED-HIGH 2½-4 min
6	HIGH 6-7 min	HIGH 5-6 min	MED-HIGH 5-6 min	MED-HIGH 4-5 min

Reheating

A cooked bacon joint is best reheated in slices (and, even better, in gravy or in a sauce). Simply arrange slices evenly on a plate and cover. In all models, cook on MEDIUM until piping hot throughout.

Baked Beans

Empty a can of beans into a dish. Cover and heat until bubbling hot, stirring occasionally.

BAKED BEANS	500W	600-700W	750-850W	900-1000W
200g can	HIGH 2-3 min	HIGH 1-2 min	MED-HIGH 1-2 min	MEDIUM 2-3 min
420g can	HIGH 4-5 min	HIGH 3-4 min	MED-HIGH 3-4 min	MED-HIGH 3-4 min

Bean Sprouts

Put the bean sprouts into a casserole (no need to add extra liquid unless you want to), cover and cook until just wilted. Use as required.

BEAN SPROUTS	500W	600-700W	750-850W	900-1000W
115g/4 oz	HIGH 2-3 min	HIGH 1-2 min	MED-HIGH 1-2 min	MED-HIGH $1/2$ to $1 1/2$ min
225g/8 oz	HIGH 3-4 min	HIGH 2-3 min	HIGH 2-3 min	HIGH $1 1/2$ to $2 1/2$ min

Beans

Frozen

Tip the frozen beans into a casserole, cover and cook until just tender, stirring occasionally.

GREEN, RUNNER, BROAD BEANS	500W	600-700W	750-850W	900-1000W
115g/4 oz	HIGH 6-8 min	HIGH 4-6 min	MED-HIGH 4-6 min	MEDIUM 6-8 min
225g/8 oz	HIGH 8-10 min	HIGH 6-8 min	MED-HIGH 6-8 min	MED-HIGH 5-7 min
450g/1 lb	HIGH 10-12 min	HIGH 8-10 min	HIGH 7-9 min	MED-HIGH 7-9 min

Fresh

Put the prepared beans into a casserole with 2-4 tbsp water. Cover and cook until just tender.

GREEN & RUNNER BEANS	500W	600-700W	750-850W	900-1000W
115g/4 oz	HIGH 6-8 min	HIGH 4-6 min	MED-HIGH 4-6 min	MEDIUM 6-8 min
225g/8 oz	HIGH 9-12 min	HIGH 7-10 min	MED-HIGH 7-10 min	MED-HIGH 6-9 min
450g/1 lb	HIGH 13-15 min	HIGH 10-12 min	HIGH 8-10 min	MED-HIGH 8-10 min

See overleaf for Broad Beans.

BROAD BEANS	500W	600-700W	750-850W	900-1000W
115g/4 oz	HIGH 4-5 min	HIGH 3-4 min	MED-HIGH 3-4 min	MED-HIGH 2-3 min
225g/8 oz	HIGH 6-8 min	HIGH 4-6 min	MED-HIGH 4-6 min	MED-HIGH 3-5 min
450g/1 lb	HIGH 8-10 min	HIGH 6-8 min	HIGH 5-7 min	MED-HIGH 5-7 min

Reheating

Put the cooked beans into a casserole and cover. In all models, simply cook on MEDIUM until hot throughout.

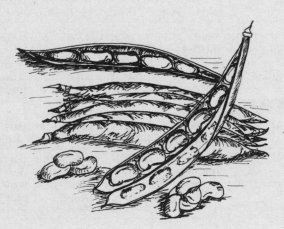

Beef

Thawing

Remove any metal ties. Stand the meat on a rack in a shallow dish or put mince into a large bowl. Cover and microwave, turning over (joints) or separating (pieces and mince) occasionally and pouring away any moisture which collects beneath the rack. Take care not to overheat beef, otherwise some parts will start to cook while other areas remain frozen. Leave joints to stand at least 30 min before cooking, steak and mince for 10 min.

BEEF	500W	600-700W	750-850W	900-1000W
joints: **per 450g/1 lb**	DEFROST 10-12 min	DEFROST 8-10 min	DEFROST 7-9 min	LOW 9-12 min
steak: **225g/8 oz**	DEFROST 8-9 min	DEFROST 6-7 min	DEFROST 5-6 min	LOW 6-8 min
per 450g/1 lb	DEFROST 10-12 min	DEFROST 8-10 min	DEFROST 7-9 min	LOW 9-12 min
cubes/mince: **115g/4 oz**	DEFROST 4-6 min	DEFROST 3-5 min	DEFROST 3-5 min	LOW 4-6 min
225g/8 oz	DEFROST 6-8 min	DEFROST 5-7 min	DEFROST 4-6 min	LOW 6-8 min
per 450g/1 lb	DEFROST 9-12 min	DEFROST 7-10 min	DEFROST 6-8 min	LOW 9-12 min

Cooking

Joints can be cooked in the microwave but, unless you have a combination microwave cooker (with convected heat as well as microwaves), you may prefer to cook them in the conventional oven. To microwave a joint, put it on a rack in a shallow dish and cover with a split microwave or roasting bag. Turn over occasionally during cooking.

Steaks are best cooked conventionally, under the grill or in a frying pan. If you do decide to cook them in the microwave, they are best cooked on a preheated browning dish – follow the manufacturer's instructions and turn the steak(s) over once during cooking.

BEEF	500W	600-700W	750-850W	900-1000W
joints: per 450g/1 lb				
– rare	HIGH 6-8 min	HIGH 5-6 min	MED-HIGH 5-6 min	MEDIUM 6-8 min
– medium	HIGH 8-10 min	HIGH 6-7 min	MED-HIGH 6-7 min	MEDIUM 8-10 min
– well done	HIGH 10-12 min	HIGH 8-9 min	MED-HIGH 8-9 min	MEDIUM 10-12 min

Reheating

A cooked beef joint is best reheated in slices (and, preferably, in gravy). Arrange slices evenly on a plate and cover. In all models, cook on MEDIUM until piping hot throughout.

Beefburgers

These are best cooked conventionally, unless you have a browning dish – in which case, follow the manufacturer's instructions.

Beetroot

Wash small or medium whole beetroot and put them into a large casserole with 150ml/¼ pt water. Cover and cook until just tender, turning them once or twice.

BEETROOT	500W	600-700W	750-850W	900-1000W
115g/4 oz	HIGH 9-11 min	HIGH 6-8 min	MED-HIGH 6-8 min	MEDIUM 9-11 min
225g/8 oz	HIGH 13-16 min	HIGH 10-12 min	MED-HIGH 10-12 min	MED-HIGH 9-11 min
450g/1 lb	HIGH 18-21 min	HIGH 14-16 min	HIGH 12-14 min	HIGH 10-12 min

Blackberries

Thawing

Put the frozen blackberries into a dish, cover and micro-wave on DEFROST, stirring gently occasionally. Leave to stand until completely thawed before using, stirring gently once or twice.

BLACKBERRIES – thawing	500W	600-700W	750-850W	900-1000W
115g/4 oz	DEFROST 1½-3 min	DEFROST 1-2 min	DEFROST 1-2 min	DEFROST ½ to 1½ min
225g/8 oz	DEFROST 4-6 min	DEFROST 3-5 min	DEFROST 2½ to 4½ min	DEFROST 2-4 min
450g/1 lb	DEFROST 8-10 min	DEFROST 6-8 min	DEFROST 5-7 min	DEFROST 4-6 min

Cooking

Put frozen or fresh blackberries into a casserole (no need to add extra liquid unless you want to), cover and cook until soft, stirring gently occasionally. Sweeten to taste.

BLACKBERRIES	500W	600-700W	750-850W	900-1000W
115g/4 oz	HIGH 2-4 min	HIGH 1-3 min	MED-HIGH 1-3 min	MEDIUM 2-4 min
225g/8 oz	HIGH 3-5 min	HIGH 2-4 min	MED-HIGH 2-4 min	MED-HIGH 2-3 min
450g/1 lb	HIGH 4-7 min	HIGH 3-6 min	HIGH 3-5 min	HIGH 3-4 min

Blackcurrants

Thawing

Put the frozen blackcurrants into a dish, cover and micro-wave on DEFROST, stirring gently occasionally. Leave to stand until completely thawed before using, stirring gently once or twice.

BLACKCURRANTS – thawing	500W	600-700W	750-850W	900-1000W
115g/4 oz	DEFROST 1½-3 min	DEFROST 1-2 min	DEFROST 1-2 min	DEFROST ½ to 1½ min
225g/8 oz	DEFROST 4-6 min	DEFROST 3-5 min	DEFROST 2½ to 4½ min	DEFROST 2-4 min
450g/1 lb	DEFROST 8-10 min	DEFROST 6-8 min	DEFROST 5-7 min	DEFROST 4-6 min

Cooking

Put frozen or fresh blackcurrants into a casserole (no need to add extra liquid unless you want to), cover and cook until just soft, stirring gently occasionally. Sweeten to taste.

BLACKCURRANTS	500W	600-700W	750-850W	900-1000W
115g/4 oz	HIGH 2-4 min	HIGH 1-3 min	MED-HIGH 1-3 min	MEDIUM 2-4 min
225g/8 oz	HIGH 3-5 min	HIGH 2-4 min	MED-HIGH 2-4 min	MED-HIGH 2-3 min
450g/1 lb	HIGH 4-7 min	HIGH 3-6 min	HIGH 3-5 min	HIGH 3-4 min

Black-eye Beans

See Pulses.

Blanching Vegetables

Blanching helps to preserve the colour, flavour and texture of vegetables which are to be frozen. Put the vegetables in a bowl with 3-4 tbsp water. Cover and cook, stirring at least once, until the vegetables are hot. Quickly drain them and plunge them into ice-cold water. Drain them again, thoroughly, then pack and freeze.

VEGETABLES for blanching	500W	600-700W	750-850W	900-1000W
225g/8 oz	HIGH 3-4 min	HIGH 2-3 min	HIGH 2 min	HIGH 1-2 min
450g/1 lb	HIGH 4-5 min	HIGH 3-4 min	HIGH 3 min	HIGH 2-3 min

Bolognese

See Sauces.

Bread

Thawing
Put the bread on a sheet of kitchen paper – it will absorb any excess moisture. Turn the bread, or separate the pieces, occasionally during microwaving. Leave to stand until completely thawed.

BREAD	500W	600-700W	750-850W	900-1000W
One 25g/1 oz slice	DEFROST 15-20 sec	DEFROST 10-15 sec	DEFROST 8-13 sec	DEFROST 7-11 sec
400g/14 oz sliced	DEFROST 6-8 min	DEFROST 4-6 min	DEFROST 4-5 min	DEFROST 4-5 min
800g/1¾ lb sliced	DEFROST 8-10 min	DEFROST 6-8 min	DEFROST 6-8 min	DEFROST 6-8 min

Breadcrumbs

Dry breadcrumbs to a golden brown in the microwave.
Use them to add colour and crunch to dishes. Spread the
fresh breadcrumbs in an even layer on an ovenproof plate
or shallow dish and heat, stirring frequently, until they
begin to colour. Keep an eye on them because, once they
begin to brown, they can easily burn.

BREADCRUMBS	500W	600-700W	750-850W	900-1000W
55g/2 oz	HIGH 3-4 min	HIGH 2-3 min	MED-HIGH 2-3 min	MEDIUM 3-4 min
75g/3 oz	HIGH 4-6 min	HIGH 3-4 min	MED-HIGH 3-4 min	MED-HIGH 2-3 min
115g/4 oz	HIGH 5-7 min	HIGH 4-5 min	HIGH 3-4 min	MED-HIGH 3-4 min

Buttered Crumbs

Crisp golden buttered crumbs make a delicious and instant topping for many dishes. Add them to salads too. Simply put some oil, or melt a little butter, in a shallow ovenproof dish first, then carefully stir in the crumbs. Cook, stirring frequently, until golden brown. The crumbs will continue to crisp up as they cool. They are best used on the day they are cooked.

BUTTERED CRUMBS	500W	600-700W	750-850W	900-1000W
55g/2 oz + 1 tbsp oil or 25g/1 oz melted butter	HIGH 3-4 min	HIGH 2-3 min	MED-HIGH 2-3 min	MEDIUM 3-4 min
75g/3 oz + 1½ tbsp oil or 40g/1½ oz melted butter	HIGH 4-6 min	HIGH 3-4 min	MED-HIGH 3-4 min	MEDIUM 4-6 min
115g/4 oz + 2 tbsp oil or 55g/2 oz melted butter	HIGH 5-7 min	HIGH 4-5 min	HIGH 3-4 min	MED-HIGH 3-4 min

Bread Rolls

Thawing

Put the frozen bread rolls on a sheet of kitchen paper – to absorb any excess moisture. Rearrange the rolls occasionally during microwaving. Leave to stand until completely thawed.

BREAD ROLLS – thawing	500W	600-700W	750-850W	900-1000W
1	DEFROST 15-20 sec	DEFROST 10-15 sec	DEFROST 8-13 sec	DEFROST 7-11 sec
2	DEFROST 20-25 sec	DEFROST 15-20 sec	DEFROST 12-18 sec	DEFROST 10-15 sec
4	DEFROST 35-40 sec	DEFROST 25-35 sec	DEFROST 22-30 sec	DEFROST 20-25 sec

Warming

Arrange the bread rolls round the edge of a plate and heat until just warm to the touch. Take care not to overheat them or the bread will be soft and rubbery. Serve immediately.

BREAD ROLLS	500W	600-700W	750-850W	900-1000W
1-2 medium	MED-HIGH 30-40 sec	MEDIUM 30-40 sec	MEDIUM 25-35 sec	MEDIUM 25-35 sec
3-4 medium	MED-HIGH $1/2$-1 min	MEDIUM 1 min	MEDIUM $1/2$-1 min	MEDIUM 35-45 sec
5-6 medium	MED-HIGH 1-2 min	MEDIUM 1-2 min	MEDIUM 1 min	MEDIUM 50-60 sec

Broccoli

Frozen

Tip the frozen florets into a casserole, cover and cook until just tender, stirring occasionally.

BROCCOLI	500W	600-700W	750-850W	900-1000W
115g/4 oz	HIGH 5-7 min	HIGH 4-6 min	MED-HIGH 4-6 min	MEDIUM 5-7 min
225g/8 oz	HIGH 8-10 min	HIGH 6-8 min	HIGH 5-7 min	MED-HIGH 5-7 min
450g/1 lb	HIGH 12-14 min	HIGH 9-11 min	HIGH 7-9 min	MED-HIGH 8-10 min

Fresh

Cut into small florets and put into a casserole with 2-4 tbsp water. Cover and cook until just tender, stirring occasionally.

BROCCOLI	500W	600-700W	750-850W	900-1000W
115g/4 oz	HIGH 4-6 min	HIGH 3-5 min	MED-HIGH 3-5 min	MEDIUM 4-6 min
225g/8 oz	HIGH 7-10 min	HIGH 5-7 min	HIGH 4-6 min	MED-HIGH 4-6 min
450g/1 lb	HIGH 9-12 min	HIGH 7-10 min	HIGH 6-8 min	MED-HIGH 6-8 min

Reheating

Put the cooked broccoli into a covered dish. In all models, cook on MEDIUM, stirring occasionally, until piping hot throughout.

Brussels Sprouts

Frozen

Tip the frozen sprouts into a casserole, cover and cook until just tender, stirring occasionally.

BRUSSELS SPROUTS	500W	600-700W	750-850W	900-1000W
115g/4 oz	HIGH 5-7 min	HIGH 4-6 min	MED-HIGH 3-5 min	MEDIUM 5-7 min
225g/8 oz	HIGH 8-10 min	HIGH 6-8 min	HIGH 5-7 min	MED-HIGH 5-7 min
450g/1 lb	HIGH 12-14 min	HIGH 9-11 min	HIGH 8-10 min	MED-HIGH 8-10 min

Fresh

Put the sprouts into a casserole with 2-4 tbsp water. Cover and cook until just tender, stirring occasionally.

BRUSSELS SPROUTS	500W	600-700W	750-850W	900-1000W
115g/4 oz	HIGH 4-5 min	HIGH 3-4 min	MED-HIGH 3-4 min	MEDIUM 4-5 min
225g/8 oz	HIGH 6-8 min	HIGH 4-6 min	HIGH 4-6 min	MED-HIGH 4-6 min
450g/1 lb	HIGH 9-12 min	HIGH 7-10 min	HIGH 5-7 min	MED-HIGH 7-9 min

Reheating

Put the cooked sprouts into a covered dish. In all models, heat on MEDIUM, stirring occasionally, until piping hot throughout.

Bulgar Wheat

Put the bulgar wheat (also called burghul or cracked wheat) into a casserole with boiling water or stock (see chart for quantities). Season with salt. Cover and cook, then leave to stand for about 5 minutes before fluffing it up with a fork and serving.

BULGAR WHEAT	500W	600-700W	750-850W	900-1000W
115g/4 oz + 300ml/½ pt boiling liquid (serves 2)	HIGH 5-7 min	HIGH 4-5 min	HIGH 3-4 min	MED-HIGH 3-4 min
225g/8 oz + 600ml/1 pt boiling liquid (serves 4)	HIGH 8-10 min	HIGH 6-8 min	HIGH 5-7 min	HIGH 4-6 min

Butter

Soften butter by heating it on MEDIUM (in a 500W cooker) or MED-LOW (in a 600-1000W cooker). Watch it carefully and stop microwaving when the butter is just soft.

To melt butter, heat on HIGH (in a 500-700W cooker) or MEDIUM (in a 750-1000W cooker). No specific times need to be followed – just stay with it and stop heating at a point when the butter has not quite finished melting, then stir well to melt it completely.

Butter Beans

See Pulses.

Cabbage

Frozen

Tip frozen chopped cabbage into a casserole, cover and cook until just tender, stirring occasionally.

CABBAGE	500W	600-700W	750-850W	900-1000W
115g/4 oz	HIGH 5-7 min	HIGH 4-6 min	MED-HIGH 4-6 min	MEDIUM 5-7 min
225g/8 oz	HIGH 8-10 min	HIGH 6-8 min	HIGH 5-7 min	MED-HIGH 5-7 min
450g/1 lb	HIGH 12-14 min	HIGH 9-11 min	HIGH 8-10 min	MED-HIGH 8-10 min

Fresh

Shred the cabbage and put it into a casserole with 2-4 tbsp water. Cover and cook until just tender, stirring occasionally.

CABBAGE	500W	600-700W	750-850W	900-1000W
115g/4 oz	HIGH 4-6 min	HIGH 3-5 min	MED-HIGH 3-5 min	MEDIUM 4-6 min
225g/8 oz	HIGH 7-10 min	HIGH 5-7 min	HIGH 4-6 min	MED-HIGH 4-6 min
450g/1 lb	HIGH 9-12 min	HIGH 7-10 min	HIGH 6-8 min	MED-HIGH 6-8 min

Reheating

See Vegetables.

Cannellini Beans

See Pulses.

Cannelloni

Thawing

Remove any foil packaging and put the cannelloni into a shallow close-fitting dish. Cover and microwave on DEFROST. Leave to stand until completely thawed.

CANNELLONI – thawing	500W	600-700W	750-850W	900-1000W
1 serving	DEFROST 5-8 min	DEFROST 4-6 min	DEFROST 4-6 min	DEFROST 3-5 min
2 servings	DEFROST 8-12 min	DEFROST 6-9 min	DEFROST 5-8 min	DEFROST 4-7 min

Reheating

Remove any foil packaging and spoon the cannelloni into a shallow close-fitting dish. Cover and cook until piping hot throughout. Leave to stand for a minute or two before serving.

CANNELLONI	500W	600-700W	750-850W	900-1000W
1 serving	HIGH 4-5 min	HIGH 3-4 min	MED-HIGH 3-4 min	MEDIUM 4-5 min
2 servings	HIGH 7-9 min	HIGH 5-7 min	MED-HIGH 5-7 min	MED-HIGH 4-6 min

Carrots

Frozen

Tip frozen carrots into a casserole, cover and cook until just tender, stirring occasionally.

CARROTS	500W	600-700W	750-850W	900-1000W
115g/4 oz	HIGH 5-7 min	HIGH 4-6 min	MED-HIGH 4-6 min	MEDIUM 5-7 min
225g/8 oz	HIGH 8-10 min	HIGH 6-8 min	HIGH 5-7 min	MED-HIGH 5-7 min
450g/1 lb	HIGH 12-14 min	HIGH 9-11 min	HIGH 8-10 min	MED-HIGH 8-10 min

Fresh

Put sliced or small whole carrots into a casserole with 2-4 tbsp water. Cover and cook until just tender, stirring occasionally.

CARROTS	500W	600-700W	750-850W	900-1000W
115g/4 oz	HIGH 5-8 min	HIGH 4-7 min	MED-HIGH 4-7 min	MEDIUM 5-8 min
225g/8 oz	HIGH 8-12 min	HIGH 7-10 min	HIGH 5-9 min	MED-HIGH 5-8 min
450g/1 lb	HIGH 12-16 min	HIGH 8-12 min	HIGH 7-10 min	MED-HIGH 7-10 min

Reheating
See Vegetables.

Casserole Dishes

Thawing

Put the food into a close-fitting dish and cover. Microwave on DEFROST, breaking up the casserole with a fork and stirring it as it thaws.

CASSEROLE – thawing	500W	600-700W	750-850W	900-1000W
1-2 servings	DEFROST 7-12 min	DEFROST 5-9 min	DEFROST 4-8 min	DEFROST 3-7 min
Family-size	DEFROST 26-32 min	DEFROST 20-25 min	DEFROST 18-22 min	DEFROST 15-20 min

Reheating

Put the food into a covered casserole. Cook, stirring occasionally, until piping hot throughout. Stir well before serving.

CASSEROLE – reheating	500W	600-700W	750-850W	900-1000W
1-2 servings	HIGH 4-6 min	HIGH 3-5 min	MED-HIGH 3-5 min	MEDIUM 4-6 min
Family-size	HIGH 12-15 min	HIGH 9-12 min	HIGH 8-11 min	MED-HIGH 7-9 min

Cauliflower

Frozen

Tip the frozen florets into a casserole, cover and cook until just tender, stirring occasionally.

CAULIFLOWER	500W	600-700W	750-850W	900-1000W
115g/4 oz	HIGH 5-7 min	HIGH 4-6 min	MED-HIGH 4-6 min	MEDIUM 5-7 min
225g/8 oz	HIGH 8-10 min	HIGH 6-8 min	HIGH 5-7 min	MED-HIGH 5-7 min
450g/1 lb	HIGH 12-14 min	HIGH 9-11 min	HIGH 8-10 min	MED-HIGH 8-10 min

Fresh

Cut the cauliflower into small florets and put them into a casserole with 2-4 tbsp water. Cover and cook until just tender, stirring occasionally.

CAULIFLOWER	500W	600-700W	750-850W	900-1000W
115g/4 oz	HIGH 4-6 min	HIGH 3-5 min	MED-HIGH 3-5 min	MEDIUM 4-6 min
225g/8 oz	HIGH 7-11 min	HIGH 5-7 min	HIGH 4-6 min	MED-HIGH 4-6 min
450g/1 lb	HIGH 9-11 min	HIGH 7-9 min	HIGH 5-7 min	MED-HIGH 5-7 min

Reheating

Put the cooked cauliflower into a covered dish. In all models, heat on MEDIUM, stirring occasionally, until piping hot throughout.

Celery

Slice thinly or cut into 2.5cm/1 in lengths and put into a casserole with 2-4 tbsp water. Cover and cook until just tender, stirring occasionally.

CELERY	500W	600-700W	750-850W	900-1000W
115g/4 oz	HIGH 5-6 min	HIGH 4-5 min	MED-HIGH 4-5 min	MEDIUM 5-6 min
225g/8 oz	HIGH 8-10 min	HIGH 6-8 min	HIGH 5-7 min	MED-HIGH 5-7 min
450g/1 lb	HIGH 10-12 min	HIGH 8-10 min	HIGH 7-9 min	MED-HIGH 7-9 min

Reheating

Put the cooked celery into a casserole and cover. In all models, simply cook on MEDIUM until hot throughout, stirring occasionally during heating.

Cheesecake

Thawing
Remove any foil packaging and put the cheesecake on a plate. Microwave on DEFROST for the time given in the chart. This method only speeds up the normal thawing process (do not try to thaw it completely in the microwave). The cheesecake must then be left to stand until it is completely thawed before serving.

CHEESECAKE	500W	600-700W	750-850W	900-1000W
15cm/6 in	DEFROST 4 min	DEFROST 3 min	DEFROST 2-3 min	DEFROST 2-3 min
20cm/8 in	DEFROST 6-8 min	DEFROST 5-6 min	DEFROST 4-5 min	DEFROST 3½ to 4½ min

Cherries

Thawing
Put the frozen cherries into a dish, cover and microwave on DEFROST, stirring gently occasionally. Leave to stand until completely thawed before using, stirring gently once or twice.

CHERRIES – thawing	500W	600-700W	750-850W	900-1000W
115g/4 oz	DEFROST 1½-3 min	DEFROST 1-2 min	DEFROST 1-2 min	DEFROST ½ to 1½ min
225g/8 oz	DEFROST 4-6 min	DEFROST 3-5 min	DEFROST 2½ to 4½ min	DEFROST 2-4 min
450g/1 lb	DEFROST 8-10 min	DEFROST 6-8 min	DEFROST 5-7 min	DEFROST 4-6 min

Cooking

Put frozen or fresh cherries into a casserole (no need to add extra liquid unless you want to), cover and cook until soft, stirring gently occasionally. Sweeten to taste.

CHERRIES	500W	600-700W	750-850W	900-1000W
115g/4 oz	HIGH 2-4 min	HIGH 1-3 min	MED-HIGH 1-3 min	MEDIUM 2-4 min
225g/8 oz	HIGH 3-5 min	HIGH 2-4 min	MED-HIGH 2-4 min	MED-HIGH 2-3 min
450g/1 lb	HIGH 4-7 min	HIGH 3-6 min	HIGH 3-5 min	HIGH 3-4 min

Chestnuts

Cook chestnuts for serving with Christmas dinner or for making stuffing. Using a sharp knife, cut a cross in the skins (to prevent them bursting open). Arrange in a single layer on an ovenproof plate or on the turntable. Cook, uncovered, removing them as they soften and peeling off their skins. Watch them carefully – if chestnuts are cooked too long, they dry up and harden.

CHESTNUTS	500W	600-700W	750-850W	900-1000W
115g/4 oz	HIGH 2-4 min	MED-HIGH 2-4 min	MEDIUM 2-4 min	MEDIUM 2-4 min
225g/8 oz	HIGH 3-5 min	HIGH 2-4 min	MED-HIGH 2-4 min	MEDIUM 3-5 min

Chick Peas

See Pulses.

Chicken

Thawing

Remove any metal ties. Stand the chicken on a rack in a shallow dish. Cover and microwave, turning over (whole birds) or separating (portions) occasionally and pouring away any moisture which collects beneath the rack. Take care not to overheat the chicken or some parts may start to cook while other areas remain frozen. Leave whole birds to stand at least 30 min before cooking, and portions for at least 10 min.

CHICKEN – thawing	500W	600-700W	750-850W	900-1000W
whole: **per 450g/1 lb**	DEFROST 8-10 min	DEFROST 6-8 min	DEFROST 5-7 min	LOW 8-10 min
portions: **225g/8 oz**	DEFROST 4-6 min	DEFROST 3-5 min	DEFROST 3-4 min	LOW 4-6 min
per 450g/1 lb	DEFROST 6-8 min	DEFROST 5-7 min	DEFROST 4-6 min	LOW 6-8 min
cubes/mince: **115g/4 oz**	DEFROST 4-6 min	DEFROST 3-5 min	DEFROST 3-4 min	LOW 4-6 min
225g/8 oz	DEFROST 6-8 min	DEFROST 5-7 min	DEFROST 4-6 min	LOW 6-8 min
per 450g/1 lb	DEFROST 9-12 min	DEFROST 7-10 min	DEFROST 6-8 min	LOW 9-12 min

Cooking

Whole birds – put on a rack in a shallow dish and cover with a split microwave or roasting bag. Turn over occasionally during cooking.

Portions – arrange in a shallow dish and add 1-2 tbsp of stock, wine, fruit juice or water. Cover and cook until tender.

CHICKEN	500W	600-700W	750-850W	900-1000W
whole: **per 450g/1 lb**	HIGH 10-13 min	HIGH 8-10 min	MED-HIGH 8-10 min	MEDIUM 10-13 min
portions – with **bone:** **225g/8 oz**	HIGH 5-7 min	HIGH 4-6 min	MED-HIGH 4-6 min	MEDIUM 5-7 min
per 450g/1 lb	HIGH 8-10 min	HIGH 6-8 min	MED-HIGH 6-8 min	MEDIUM 8-10 min
boneless breasts: **1**	HIGH 3-4 min	HIGH 2-3 min	MED-HIGH 2-3 min	MEDIUM 3-4 min
2	HIGH 4-6 min	HIGH 3-5 min	MED-HIGH 3-5 min	MEDIUM 4-6 min
3	HIGH 5-7 min	HIGH 4-6 min	MED-HIGH 4-6 min	MEDIUM 5-7 min
4	HIGH 6-8 min	HIGH 5-7 min	MED-HIGH 5-7 min	MEDIUM 6-8 min

Reheating
Cooked chicken is best reheated in pieces (and, preferably, in a sauce). Arrange pieces, in an even layer, in a shallow dish and cover. In all models, cook on MEDIUM until piping hot throughout.

Chips

It is not possible to cook chips successfully in a microwave, unless you buy the ready-prepared products which are specifically made for the purpose – in which case, follow the instructions on the packet.

Chocolate

Melt as little, or as much, chocolate as you need. Break the chocolate into small pieces and put them in a bowl (alternatively, use chocolate drops). The melting time will vary from brand to brand, so just heat on MED-HIGH (in a 500W cooker), MEDIUM (in a 600-700W cooker) or MED-LOW (in a 750-1000W cooker), stirring frequently, until the chocolate softens and becomes glossy. Stir it well until it has melted completely. Check the chocolate often – if it overheats, it will harden and burn.

Chops

See Bacon, Lamb, Pork.

Christmas Pudding

Reheating

Christmas puddings are usually high in fat, sugar and alcohol – all of which, if overheated, can easily burn. Follow the microwave heating times on the pack, or use this chart as a guide. Best results are obtained using MEDIUM or a lower power. Either leave the pudding in the dish or (particularly if the pudding is in a foil container) invert it on to an ovenproof plate and cover. A single portion can be heated in a serving bowl. Cover and heat until soft and piping hot throughout. Leave to stand for 3-5 min (whole pudding) or 1-2 min (single portion) before serving.

CHRISTMAS PUDDING	500W	600-700W	750-850W	900-1000W
1 serving	MEDIUM 1-2 min	MEDIUM 1 min	MED-LOW 1-2 min	MED-LOW $1/2$ to $1 1/2$ min
450g/1 lb	MEDIUM 4-7 min	MEDIUM 3-5 min	MEDIUM 3-4 min	MEDIUM 3-4 min
900g/2 lb	MEDIUM 11-15 min	MEDIUM 8-12 min	MEDIUM 7-10 min	MEDIUM 6-8 min

Coconut

'Toast' coconut in the microwave by spreading an even layer in a shallow dish. Cook, uncovered and stirring frequently, on HIGH (in a 500-700W cooker) or MEDIUM (in a 750-1000W cooker) until the coconut just turns golden brown.

Cod

See Fish.

Coffee

Making instant coffee in the microwave is handy if you are making only one or two cups. Pour cold water into a cup or mug (about 200ml/7 fl oz) and heat, stirring once or twice, until it just begins to bubble. Stir the water well, then add the coffee powder or granules.

COFFEE	500W	600-700W	750-850W	900-1000W
1 x 200ml/7 fl oz	HIGH 2-3 min	HIGH 1½-2 min	MED-HIGH 1½-2 min	MED-HIGH 1-1½ min
2 x 200ml/7 fl oz	HIGH 3-4 min	HIGH 2-3 min	MED-HIGH 2-3 min	MED-HIGH 2-3 min

Reheating

Coffee that has gone cold can be reheated in the micro-wave. Pour into cups or mugs (about 200ml/7 fl oz in each) and heat, stirring once or twice, until piping hot but not quite boiling. Stir again before serving.

COFFEE	500W	600-700W	750-850W	900-1000W
1 x 200ml/7 fl oz	HIGH 2-3 min	HIGH 1½-2 min	MED-HIGH 1½-2 min	MED-HIGH 1-1½ min
2 x 200ml/7 fl oz	HIGH 3-4 min	HIGH 2-3 min	MED-HIGH 2-3 min	MED-HIGH 2-3 min
4 x 200ml/7 fl oz	HIGH 4-6 min	HIGH 3-5 min	MED-HIGH 3-5 min	MED-HIGH 3-4 min

Corn on the Cob

Frozen
Put the frozen cobs into a casserole, cover and cook until just tender, turning occasionally.

CORN ON THE COB	500W	600-700W	750-850W	900-1000W
1	HIGH 4-5 min	HIGH 3-4 min	MED-HIGH 3-4 min	MEDIUM 4-5 min
2	HIGH 8-10 min	HIGH 6-8 min	HIGH 5-7 min	MED-HIGH 5-7 min

Fresh
Put the cobs into a large casserole with 2-4 tbsp water. Cover and cook until just tender, turning occasionally.

CORN ON THE COB	500W	600-700W	750-850W	900-1000W
1	HIGH 4-5 min	HIGH 3-4 min	MED-HIGH 3-4 min	MEDIUM 4-5 min
2	HIGH 8-10 min	HIGH 6-8 min	HIGH 5-7 min	MED-HIGH 5-7 min

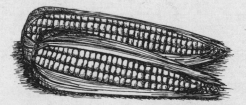

Courgettes

Frozen
Put the courgettes into a casserole, cover and cook until just tender, stirring occasionally.

COURGETTES	500W	600-700W	750-850W	900-1000W
115g/4 oz	HIGH 3-4 min	HIGH 2-3 min	MED-HIGH 2-3 min	MEDIUM 3-4 min
225g/8 oz	HIGH 4-5 min	HIGH 3-4 min	HIGH 3-4 min	MED-HIGH 3-4 min
450g/1 lb	HIGH 6-8 min	HIGH 5-7 min	HIGH 4-6 min	MED-HIGH 4-6 min

Fresh
Put sliced or small whole courgettes into a casserole with 2-4 tbsp water. Cover and cook until just tender, stirring occasionally.

COURGETTES	500W	600-700W	750-850W	900-1000W
115g/4 oz	HIGH 3-4 min	HIGH 2-3 min	MED-HIGH 2-3 min	MEDIUM 3-4 min
225g/8 oz	HIGH 4-5 min	HIGH 3-4 min	HIGH 3-4 min	MED-HIGH 3-4 min
450g/1 lb	HIGH 6-8 min	HIGH 5-7 min	HIGH 4-6 min	MED-HIGH 4-6 min

Reheating
Put the cooked courgettes into a covered dish. In all models, cook on MEDIUM, stirring occasionally, until piping hot throughout.

Couscous

Put the couscous into a casserole with oil and boiling water or stock (see chart for quantities). Season with salt. Cover and cook, then leave to stand for about 5 minutes before stirring it with a fork and serving.

COUSCOUS	500W	600-700W	750-850W	900-1000W
115g/4 oz + 1 tbsp olive oil + 300ml/½ pt boiling liquid (serves 2)	HIGH 4-5 min	HIGH 3-4 min	HIGH 2½ to 3½ min	MED-HIGH 3-4 min
225g/8 oz + 2 tbsp olive oil + 600ml/1 pt boiling liquid (serves 4)	HIGH 6-8 min	HIGH 4-6 min	HIGH 3-5 min	HIGH 2-4 min

Croissants

Thawing
Put the frozen croissants on a sheet of kitchen paper. Rearrange them occasionally during microwaving. Take care not to overheat them. Leave to stand until completely thawed.

CROISSANTS – thawing	500W	600-700W	750-850W	900-1000W
1	DEFROST 20 sec	DEFROST 15 sec	DEFROST 13-14 sec	DEFROST 12 sec
2	DEFROST 40 sec	DEFROST 30 sec	DEFROST 25 sec	DEFROST 20-25 sec
4	DEFROST 1-1½ min	DEFROST 1 min	DEFROST ½-1 min	DEFROST ½-1 min

Warming
Arrange the croissants round the edge of a plate and heat until just warm to the touch. Take care not to overheat them or the croissants will be soggy. Serve immediately.

CROISSANTS	500W	600-700W	750-850W	900-1000W
1-2	MED-HIGH 30-40 sec	MEDIUM 30-40 sec	MEDIUM 25-35 sec	MEDIUM 25-35 sec
3-4	MED-HIGH ½-1 min	MEDIUM 1 min	MEDIUM ½-1 min	MEDIUM 35-45 sec

Croûtons

Croûtons provide a crunchy garnish for soups and make a delicious addition to salads. Spread bread slices thinly on both sides with softened plain, garlic or herb butter. Alternatively, brush them with oil. Trim off the crusts and cut the remaining bread into 1cm/½ in cubes. Spread the cubes, in a single layer, on an ovenproof plate and cook, stirring occasionally, until golden brown. They will continue to crisp up as they cool and are best used on the day they are made.

CROÛTONS	500W	600-700W	750-850W	900-1000W
1 bread slice	HIGH 2-3 min	HIGH 1-2 min	MED-HIGH 1-2 min	MEDIUM 2-3 min
2 bread slices	HIGH 3-4 min	HIGH 2-3 min	HIGH 2-3 min	MED-HIGH 2-3 min
3 bread slices	HIGH 4-5 min	HIGH 3-4 min	HIGH 3-4 min	MED-HIGH 3-4 min

Curry

See Casserole Dishes.

Custard

No specific cooking times need to be followed for making custard. In a large jug or bowl, mix the custard powder with a little milk to make a smooth paste, then stir in the remaining milk. In all models, cook on HIGH, stirring or whisking frequently, until the custard boils and thickens and is velvety smooth. Sweeten to taste and serve. Nothing could be more simple!

Reheating
Pour the custard into a jug or bowl and heat until bubbling hot, stirring once or twice.

CUSTARD	500W	600-700W	750-850W	900-1000W
150ml/¼ pt	HIGH 2-3 min	HIGH 1-2 min	MED-HIGH 1-2 min	MED-HIGH 1 min
300ml/½ pt	HIGH 3-4 min	HIGH 2-3 min	HIGH 1-2 min	MED-HIGH 1-2 min
600ml/1 pt	HIGH 4-5 min	HIGH 3-4 min	HIGH 2-3 min	MED-HIGH 2-3 min

Dried Fruit

Cook dried fruit such as apricots, prunes, pears, apples or a mixture. Put the fruit into a casserole and pour over fruit juice, tea (without milk) or water (see chart for quantities). For a winter fruit salad, add a little vanilla essence, a cinnamon stick and a few whole cloves. Cover and cook, stirring occasionally, until the fruit is plump and tender. Sweeten to taste with sugar or honey and leave to stand for at least 5 minutes. Serve hot or at room temperature as a dessert with a spoonful of whipped cream or Greek yogurt. It's also delicious served chilled for breakfast.

DRIED FRUIT	500W	600-700W	750-850W	900-1000W
115g/4 oz + 150ml/¼ pt liquid	HIGH 8-10 min	HIGH 6-8 min	MED-HIGH 6-8 min	MEDIUM 8-10 min
225g/8 oz + 300ml/½ pt liquid	HIGH 13-15 min	HIGH 10-12 min	HIGH 8-10 min	HIGH 7-9 min

Drinks

See Coffee, Milk, Tea.

Duck

Thawing

Remove any metal ties. Stand the duck on a rack in a shallow dish. Cover and microwave, turning over (whole birds) or separating (portions) occasionally and pouring away any moisture which collects beneath the rack. Leave whole birds to stand at least 30 min before cooking, and portions for at least 10 min.

DUCK – thawing	500W	600-700W	750-850W	900-1000W
whole or portions: per 450g/1 lb	DEFROST 6-9 min	DEFROST 5-7 min	DEFROST 4-6 min	LOW 6-10 min

Cooking

A whole duck can be cooked in the microwave but, unless you have a combination microwave cooker (with convected heat as well as microwaves), you may prefer to cook it in the conventional oven. If you decide to use the microwave, put the duck on a rack in a shallow ovenproof dish and cover with a split microwave or roasting bag. Turn over occasionally during cooking, pouring away any excess fat.

DUCK	500W	600-700W	750-850W	900-1000W
whole: **per 450g/1 lb**	HIGH 9-12 min	HIGH 7-10 min	MED-HIGH 7-10 min	MEDIUM 9-12 min
175g/6 oz **portions: 1**	HIGH 3-5 min	MEDIUM 4-6 min	MEDIUM 4-6 min	MEDIUM 3-5 min
2	HIGH 4-7 min	MEDIUM 6-8 min	MEDIUM 6-8 min	MEDIUM 4-6 min
3	HIGH 6-9 min	MED-HIGH 6-8 min	MEDIUM 8-10 min	MEDIUM 6-8 min
4	HIGH 8-10 min	MED-HIGH 7-9 min	MEDIUM 10-12 min	MEDIUM 8-10 min

Reheating

Duck is best reheated in pieces (and, preferably, in a sauce). Arrange pieces, in an even layer, in a shallow dish and cover. In all models, cook on MEDIUM until piping hot throughout.

Eggs

Eggs cook best in the microwave if they are removed from the refrigerator and allowed to come to room temperature first.

Baked
Break medium eggs into small ramekins, dishes or cups. Prick the yolks in a few places. Arrange the ramekins, in a circle, in the microwave. Cook until almost set then leave to stand for a minute or two before serving while they finish setting. Run a knife around the edge and slide the eggs on to hot buttered toast.

BAKED EGGS	500W	600-700W	750-850W	900-1000W
1	HIGH 1½ min	HIGH 1 min	MED-HIGH 1 min	MEDIUM 1½ min
2	HIGH 2 min	HIGH 1½ min	MED-HIGH 1½ min	MEDIUM 2 min
3	HIGH 2½ min	HIGH 2 min	MED-HIGH 2 min	MEDIUM 2½ min
4	HIGH 3-3½ min	HIGH 2½ min	MED-HIGH 2½ min	MED-HIGH 1½-2 min

Poached
Poaching an egg in water is only worth doing if you are cooking one egg. Pour 150ml/¼ pt water into a medium bowl or jug and add a dash of vinegar. Heat on HIGH, stirring once,

until just boiling. Break a medium egg into the boiling water and prick the yolk (a cocktail stick is handy for this). Cook until the water just starts to bubble around the edges (normally 20-60 sec), then leave to stand for a min or two while the egg finishes setting. When it is done to your liking, lift it out with a slotted spoon and serve on hot buttered toast.

Scrambled

Crack medium eggs into a bowl or jug and beat well. Stir in a little milk, seasoning and a knob of butter. Cook, stirring frequently (each time the egg mixture begins to set around the edge of the bowl) until they are nearly cooked to your liking. Leave to stand for a minute and they will set a little more. Spoon the eggs on to hot buttered toast.

SCRAMBLED EGGS	500W	600-700W	750-850W	900-1000W
2 medium eggs + 2 tbsp milk, seasoning, knob of butter	HIGH 2-3 min	HIGH 1½-2 min	MED-HIGH 1-2 min	MEDIUM 2-3 min
4 medium eggs + 4 tbsp milk, seasoning, knob of butter	HIGH 3-4½ min	HIGH 2½ to 3½ min	MED-HIGH 2½ to 3½ min	MED-HIGH 2-3 min

Fennel

Slice or cut the fennel into thin wedges and put them into a casserole with 2-4 tbsp water. Cover and cook until just tender, stirring occasionally.

FENNEL	500W	600-700W	750-850W	900-1000W
115g/4 oz	HIGH 4-5 min	HIGH 3-4 min	MED-HIGH 3-4 min	MED-HIGH 3-4 min
225g/8 oz	HIGH 7-8 min	HIGH 5-6 min	HIGH 3-4 min	MED-HIGH 3-4 min
450g/1 lb	HIGH 9-11 min	HIGH 7-8 min	HIGH 4-5 min	MED-HIGH 4-5 min

Fish

Thawing

Remove any metal ties and put the fish in a shallow dish. Cover and microwave – separating, repositioning and removing pieces as they thaw. Take care not to overheat fish. If you do, it will begin to cook in some areas, while other parts remain frozen. Once thawed, leave to stand for 5-10 min before cooking.

FISH – thawing	500W	600-700W	750-850W	900-1000W
whole round (trout, mackerel, mullet):				
225g/8 oz	DEFROST 3-5 min	DEFROST 2-4 min	DEFROST 2-3 min	DEFROST 2-3 min
per 450g/1 lb	DEFROST 5-7 min	DEFROST 4-6 min	DEFROST 3-5 min	DEFROST 3-4 min
whole flat fish (plaice, sole), cutlets, steaks, fillets:				
225g/8 oz	DEFROST 3-4 min	DEFROST 2-3 min	DEFROST 1-2 min	DEFROST 1-2 min
per 450g/1 lb	DEFROST 4-5 min	DEFROST 3-4 min	DEFROST 2-3 min	DEFROST 2-3 min
prawns, shrimps:				
115g/4 oz	DEFROST 3-4 min	DEFROST 2-3 min	DEFROST 1-2 min	DEFROST 1-2 min
225g/8 oz	DEFROST 5-7 min	DEFROST 3-4 min	DEFROST 2-3 min	DEFROST 2-3 min
scallops:				
225g/8 oz	DEFROST 5-7 min	DEFROST 3-4 min	DEFROST 2-3 min	DEFROST 2-3 min

Cooking

Make a few slits in the skin of whole fish. Arrange in an even layer in a shallow dish. Either brush fillets or whole fish with melted butter or add a tablespoon or two of wine, fruit juice, water or milk. Mussels need 150ml/¼ pt wine stock or water. Cover and cook, turning whole fish over once during cooking. Stir or shake small pieces (such as prawns, scallops and mussels) frequently. It's better to undercook fish slightly, until the thick flakes are still slightly translucent. Just leave it to stand, covered, for a few minutes and it will finish cooking to perfection.

If you find that fish tends to spit and overcook on the edges, a better result is usually achieved by lowering the power level slightly and cooking for a little longer.

FISH	500W	600-700W	750-850W	900-1000W
whole round (trout, mackerel, mullet):				
225g/8 oz	HIGH 3-4 min	HIGH 3 min	MEDIUM 4 min	MEDIUM 3-4 min
per 450g/1 lb	HIGH 5 min	HIGH 4 min	MEDIUM 6 min	MEDIUM 5 min
whole flat (plaice, sole):				
225g/8 oz	HIGH 3 min	HIGH 2 min	MEDIUM 2-3 min	MEDIUM 2-3 min
per 450g/1 lb	HIGH 4 min	HIGH 3 min	MEDIUM 5 min	MEDIUM 4 min
steaks, cutlets, thick fillets (such as cod, haddock, salmon):				
225g/8 oz	HIGH 3-5 min	HIGH 3-4 min	MEDIUM 4-5 min	MEDIUM 3-5 min
per 450g/1 lb	HIGH 5-8 min	HIGH 4-6 min	MEDIUM 5-7 min	MEDIUM 5-7 min

FISH	500W	600-700W	750-850W	900-1000W
thin fillets:				
225g/8 oz	HIGH 2-3 min	HIGH 1-2 min	MEDIUM 2-3 min	MEDIUM 2-3 min
per 450g/1 lb	HIGH 3-4 min	HIGH 2-3 min	MEDIUM 3-4 min	MEDIUM 3-4 min
prawns – raw:				
115g/4 oz	MEDIUM 4 min	MEDIUM 3 min	MEDIUM 2-3 min	MEDIUM 2-3 min
225g/8 oz	HIGH 4 min	HIGH 2-3 min	MEDIUM 3-4 min	MEDIUM 3-4 min
450g/1 lb	HIGH 3-5 min	HIGH 2-4 min	MED-HIGH 2-4 min	MEDIUM 3-5 min
scallops:				
450g/lb	HIGH 3-5 min	HIGH 2-4 min	MED-HIGH 2-4 min	MEDIUM 3-5 min
mussels:				
450g/1 lb	HIGH 3-4 min	HIGH 2-4 min	HIGH 2-4 min	MED-HIGH 2-4 min
900g/2 lb	HIGH 4-6 min	HIGH 3-5 min	HIGH 3-5 min	MED-HIGH 2-4 min

Reheating
Fish is not suitable for reheating.

Fish Fingers

These are not really suitable for cooking in the microwave, unless you have a browning dish – in which case, follow the manufacturer's instructions.

Flageolet Beans

See Pulses.

Flan – Savoury

Thawing
Remove any foil packaging and put the flan on a plate. Take care not to overheat it. Leave to stand for a minute or two before serving or reheating.

FLAN	500W	600-700W	750-850W	900-1000W
1 serving	DEFROST 3-4 min	DEFROST 2$\frac{1}{2}$-3 min	DEFROST 2-2$\frac{1}{2}$ min	DEFROST 2-2$\frac{1}{2}$ min
Family-size	DEFROST 10-12 min	DEFROST 8-10 min	DEFROST 7-9 min	DEFROST 6-8 min

Reheating
Put the flan on a serving plate and cook until hot through-out. The pastry will not remain crisp. Leave to stand for a minute or two before serving.

FLAN	500W	600-700W	750-850W	900-1000W
1 serving	MEDIUM 1-1$\frac{1}{2}$ min	MEDIUM $\frac{1}{2}$-1 min	MED-LOW $\frac{1}{2}$-1 min	MED-LOW $\frac{1}{2}$-1 min
Family-size	MED-HIGH 3$\frac{1}{2}$-5 min	MEDIUM 3$\frac{1}{2}$-5 min	MEDIUM 3-4 min	MED-LOW 3-4 min

Fruit

See individual entries and Pies.

Fruit – Dried

See Dried Fruit.

Gammon

See Bacon.

Globe Artichokes

See Artichokes.

Gooseberries

Put frozen or fresh gooseberries into a casserole (no need to add extra liquid unless you want to), cover and cook until just soft, stirring gently occasionally. Sweeten to taste and leave to stand for a few minutes.

GOOSEBERRIES	500W	600-700W	750-850W	900-1000W
115g/4 oz	HIGH 2-4 min	HIGH 1-3 min	MED-HIGH 1-3 min	MEDIUM 2-4 min
225g/8 oz	HIGH 3-5 min	HIGH 2-4 min	MED-HIGH 2-4 min	MED-HIGH 2-3 min
450g/1 lb	HIGH 4-7 min	HIGH 3-6 min	HIGH 3-5 min	HIGH 2-4 min

Gravy

Thawing
Put the frozen gravy into a bowl or jug and microwave on DEFROST, breaking it up with a fork as it thaws.

GRAVY – thawing	500W	600-700W	750-850W	900-1000W
150ml/¼ pt	DEFROST 8-10 min	DEFROST 6-8 min	DEFROST 5-7 min	DEFROST 5-6 min
300ml/½ pt	DEFROST 12-15 min	DEFROST 8-12 min	DEFROST 7-10 min	DEFROST 6-8 min
600ml/1 pt	DEFROST 15-20 min	DEFROST 12-15 min	DEFROST 10-12 min	DEFROST 9-11 min

Reheating
Put the gravy into a bowl or jug and heat, stirring occasionally, until bubbling hot.

GRAVY	500W	600-700W	750-850W	900-1000W
150ml/¼ pt	HIGH 2½-3 min	HIGH 2 min	MED-HIGH 2 min	MEDIUM 2½-3 min
300ml/½ pt	HIGH 4 min	HIGH 3 min	MED-HIGH 3 min	MED-HIGH 2-3 min
600ml/1 pt	HIGH 7-9 min	HIGH 5-7 min	HIGH 4-6 min	HIGH 3½-5 min

Haddock

See Fish.

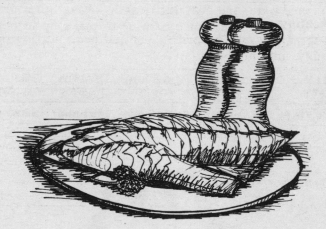

Haricot Beans

See Pulses.

Jelly

Break a fruit jelly tablet into squares and put them into a measuring jug which holds at least 600ml/1 pt. Add 150ml/ ¼ pt cold water and heat until just dissolved. Stir well then add cold water, fruit juice or wine to make up to 600ml/ 1 pt. Chill to set.

JELLY	500W	600-700W	750-850W	900-1000W
140g	HIGH 2 min	HIGH 1½ min	MED-HIGH 1½ min	HIGH 50-60 sec

Jerusalem Artichokes

See Artichokes.

Kidney Beans

See Pulses.

Kidneys

Thawing

Put the kidneys in a dish, cover and microwave, separating them as they thaw. Take care not to overheat kidneys, otherwise some parts may begin to cook while other areas remain frozen. Leave to stand for 5-10 min before cooking.

KIDNEYS – thawing	500W	600-700W	750-850W	900-1000W
225g/8 oz	DEFROST 6-7 min	DEFROST 5-6 min	DEFROST 4-5 min	DEFROST $3^1/_2$ to $4^1/_2$ min
per 450g/1 lb	DEFROST 9-12 min	DEFROST 7-9 min	DEFROST 6-8 min	DEFROST 5-7 min

Cooking

Kidneys are best cooked in a sauce, chopped or sliced first. Cooking times will depend on the type and quantity of kidney and the sauce used. In all models, simply cover and bring to the boil on HIGH, then continue cooking on MEDIUM, stirring occasionally, until the kidneys are tender.

Reheating

Kidneys are best reheated in a sauce. In all models, simply cover and cook on MEDIUM until piping hot throughout, stirring occasionally.

Lamb

Thawing

Remove any metal ties. Stand the meat on a rack in a shallow dish or put mince into a large bowl. Cover and microwave, turning over (joints) or separating (pieces and mince) occasionally and pouring away any moisture which collects beneath the rack. Take care not to overheat the lamb, otherwise some parts may begin to cook while other areas remain frozen. Leave joints to stand at least 30 min before cooking, chops and mince for 10 min.

LAMB – thawing	500W	600-700W	750-850W	900-1000W
joints: **per 450g/1 lb**	DEFROST 6-7 min	DEFROST 5-6 min	DEFROST 4-5 min	LOW 6-8 min
chops: **225g/8 oz**	DEFROST 7-9 min	DEFROST 6-7 min	DEFROST 5-6 min	LOW 6-8 min
per 450g/1 lb	DEFROST 10-12 min	DEFROST 8-10 min	DEFROST 7-9 min	LOW 9-12 min
cubes/mince: **115g/4 oz**	DEFROST 4-6 min	DEFROST 3-5 min	DEFROST 3-4 min	LOW 4-6 min
225g/8 oz	DEFROST 6-8 min	DEFROST 5-7 min	DEFROST 4-6 min	LOW 6-8 min
per 450g/1 lb	DEFROST 9-12 min	DEFROST 7-10 min	DEFROST 6-8 min	LOW 9-12 min

Cooking

Joints can be cooked in the microwave but, unless you have a combination microwave cooker (with convected heat as well as microwaves), you may prefer to cook them in the conventional oven. To microwave a joint, put it on a rack in a shallow dish and cover with a split microwave or roasting bag. Turn over occasionally during cooking.

Chops are best cooked on a preheated browning dish – follow the manufacturer's instructions and turn the chops over once during cooking.

LAMB	500W	600-700W	750-850W	900-1000W
joints: **per 450g/1 lb** **– medium** – well done	HIGH 9-11 min HIGH 10-12 min	HIGH 7-8 min HIGH 8-10 min	MED-HIGH 7-8 min MED-HIGH 8-10 min	MEDIUM 9-11 min MEDIUM 10-12 min
chops: 1 2 3 4	HIGH 3-5 min HIGH 4-6 min HIGH 5-7 min HIGH 6-8 min	HIGH 2-4 min HIGH 3-5 min HIGH 4-6 min HIGH 5-7 min	MED-HIGH 2-4 min MED-HIGH 3-5 min MED-HIGH 4-6 min MED-HIGH 5-7 min	MEDIUM 3-5 min MEDIUM 4-6 min MEDIUM 5-7 min MEDIUM 6-8 min

Reheating

A cooked lamb joint is best reheated in slices (and, even better, in gravy). Arrange slices evenly on a plate and cover. In all models, cook on MEDIUM until piping hot throughout.

Lasagne

Thawing

Remove any foil packaging and put into a close-fitting dish. Cover and microwave. Leave to stand for 10-15 min before reheating.

LASAGNE – thawing	500W	600-700W	750-850W	900-1000W
1 serving	DEFROST 9-11 min	DEFROST 7-8 min	DEFROST 6-7 min	DEFROST 5-6 min
Family-size	DEFROST 13-19 min	DEFROST 10-15 min	DEFROST 8-12 min	DEFROST 7-11 min

Reheating

Remove any foil packaging and put into a close-fitting dish. With a sharp knife, pierce the lasagne in several places – to help it to heat evenly. Cover and cook until piping hot throughout. Leave to stand for 3-5 min before serving.

LASAGNE	500W	600-700W	750-850W	900-1000W
1 serving	HIGH 3-4 min	MEDIUM 4-6 min	MEDIUM 4-5 min	MEDIUM 3-4 min
Family-size	HIGH 10-15 min	MEDIUM 15-20 min	MEDIUM 12-17 min	MEDIUM 10-15 min

Leeks

Frozen
Tip the frozen leeks into a casserole, cover and cook until just tender, stirring occasionally.

LEEKS	500W	600-700W	750-850W	900-1000W
115g/4 oz	HIGH 3-4 min	HIGH 2-3 min	MED-HIGH 2-3 min	MED-HIGH $1\frac{1}{2}$ to $2\frac{1}{2}$ min
225g/8 oz	HIGH 4-6 min	HIGH 3-5 min	HIGH 2-4 min	MED-HIGH 2-4 min
450g/1 lb	HIGH 6-9 min	HIGH 5-7 min	HIGH 4-6 min	HIGH $3\frac{1}{2}$ to $5\frac{1}{2}$ min

Fresh
Put sliced or whole baby leeks into a casserole and add 2-4 tbsp water. Cover and cook until just tender, stirring or rearranging occasionally.

LEEKS	500W	600-700W	750-850W	900-1000W
115g/4 oz	HIGH 4-5 min	HIGH 3-4 min	MED-HIGH 3-4 min	MED-HIGH 2-3 min
225g/8 oz	HIGH 6-8 min	HIGH 4-6 min	HIGH 3-5 min	MED-HIGH 3-5 min
450g/1 lb	HIGH 9-11 min	HIGH 6-8 min	HIGH 5-7 min	MED-HIGH 5-7 min

Reheating
Put the leeks in a dish and cover. In all models, simply cook on MED-HIGH until hot throughout, stirring occasionally.

Lemons

See Oranges and Lemons.

Lentils

See Pulses.

Liver

Thawing
Put the liver in a dish, cover and microwave, separating the pieces as they thaw. Take care not to overheat liver, otherwise some parts may begin to cook while other areas remain frozen. Leave to stand for 5-10 min before cooking.

LIVER – thawing	500W	600-700W	750-850W	900-1000W
225g/8 oz	DEFROST 6-7 min	DEFROST 5-6 min	DEFROST 4-5 min	DEFROST 3½ to 4½ min
per 450g/1 lb	DEFROST 9-12 min	DEFROST 7-9 min	DEFROST 6-8 min	DEFROST 5-7 min

Cooking
For best results, cut or slice liver into bite-size pieces and cook in a sauce. Cooking times will depend on the type and quantity of liver and the sauce used. In all models, simply cover and bring to the boil on HIGH, then continue cooking on MEDIUM, stirring occasionally, until tender.

Reheating
Liver is best reheated in a sauce. In all models, simply cover and cook on MEDIUM until piping hot throughout, stirring occasionally.

Mackerel

See Fish.

Mange-tout

Frozen
Tip the frozen mange-tout into a casserole. Cover and cook until just tender, stirring occasionally.

MANGE-TOUT	500W	600-700W	750-850W	900-1000W
115g/4 oz	HIGH 4-5 min	HIGH 3-4 min	MED-HIGH 3-4 min	MED-HIGH 3-4 min
225g/8 oz	HIGH 7-8 min	HIGH 5-6 min	HIGH 3-4 min	MED-HIGH 3-4 min
450g/1 lb	HIGH 9-11 min	HIGH 7-8 min	HIGH 4-5 min	MED-HIGH 4-5 min

Fresh
Put the mange-tout into a casserole with 2-4 tbsp water. Cover and cook until just tender, stirring occasionally.

MANGE-TOUT	500W	600-700W	750-850W	900-1000W
115g/4 oz	HIGH 4-5 min	HIGH 3-4 min	MED-HIGH 3-4 min	MED-HIGH 3-4 min
225g/8 oz	HIGH 7-8 min	HIGH 5-6 min	HIGH 3-4 min	MED-HIGH 3-4 min
450g/1 lb	HIGH 9-11 min	HIGH 7-8 min	HIGH 4-5 min	MED-HIGH 4-5 min

Reheating

Put the cooked mange-tout into a covered dish. In all models, heat on MEDIUM, stirring occasionally, until piping hot.

Marrow

Peel and halve the marrow lengthways, remove the seeds and cut the flesh into bite-size cubes. Put into a casserole with 2-4 tbsp water. Cover and cook until just tender, stirring gently occasionally.

MARROW	500W	600-700W	750-850W	900-1000W
115g/4 oz	HIGH 4-5 min	HIGH 3-4 min	MED-HIGH 3-4 min	MED-HIGH 3-4 min
225g/8 oz	HIGH 6-8 min	HIGH 5-6 min	HIGH 4-5 min	MED-HIGH 4-5 min
450g/1 lb	HIGH 8-10 min	HIGH 6-8 min	HIGH 5-7 min	MED-HIGH 5-7 min

Reheating

Cooked marrow is best reheated in a sauce. In all models, simply cover and cook on MEDIUM until hot throughout, stirring occasionally.

Meat Loaf

Thawing
The thawing time will depend on the shape and size, together with the type of meat used. Simply microwave on DEFROST. Stop microwaving when any part of the loaf becomes slightly warm. Leave to stand until completely thawed.

Reheating
Reheat meat loaf whole or in slices. In all models, simply cover and cook on MEDIUM until piping hot throughout, turning the loaf or rearranging slices occasionally.

Milk

The microwave is ideal for warming milk for drinks, particularly if you are making just one or two cups. Pour cold milk into a cup(s) or mug(s) – about 200ml/7 fl oz in each – and heat, stirring once or twice, until bubbles begin to form below its surface. Stir the milk and serve as it is or with a flavouring stirred in. Take care not to overheat it or it will boil over.

MILK	500W	600-700W	750-850W	900-1000W
1 x 200ml/7 fl oz	HIGH 1½-2 min	HIGH 1-1½ min	MED-HIGH 1-1½ min	MEDIUM 1½-2 min
2 x 200ml/7 fl oz	HIGH 2½-4 min	HIGH 1½-3 min	MED-HIGH 1½-3 min	MEDIUM 2½-4 min

Mince

See Beef, Chicken, Lamb, Pork.

Mince Pies

Reheating
Remove any foil packaging and arrange the pies on a microwave rack. Using a small sharp knife, pierce each pastry lid once. Heat until the pastry just feels warm (the filling will be much hotter than the pastry). Take care – if mince pies are overheated the filling will be burning hot and pastry will be soggy.

MINCE PIES	500W	600-700W	750-850W	900-1000W
2	MED-HIGH 1 min	MEDIUM $1/2$-1 min	MED-LOW $1/2$-1 min	MED-LOW $1/2$-1 min
4	MED-HIGH 1-2 min	MEDIUM 1-2 min	MEDIUM 1-2 min	MEDIUM $1/2$ to $1^1/2$ min
6	MED-HIGH 2-3 min	MEDIUM 2-3 min	MEDIUM 1-2 min	MEDIUM 1-2 min

Moussaka

Thawing

Remove any foil packaging and put into a close-fitting dish. Cover and microwave on DEFROST. Leave to stand for 10-15 min before reheating.

MOUSSAKA – thawing	500W	600-700W	750-850W	900-1000W
1 serving	DEFROST 9-11 min	DEFROST 7-8 min	DEFROST 6-7 min	DEFROST 5-6 min
Family-size	DEFROST 13-19 min	DEFROST 10-15 min	DEFROST 8-12 min	DEFROST 7-11 min

Reheating

Remove any foil packaging and put into a close-fitting dish. With a sharp knife, pierce the moussaka in several places – to help it to heat evenly. Cover and cook until piping hot throughout. Leave to stand for 3-5 min before serving.

MOUSSAKA	500W	600-700W	750-850W	900-1000W
1 serving	HIGH 3-4 min	MEDIUM 4-6 min	MEDIUM 4-5 min	MEDIUM 3-4 min
Family-size	HIGH 10-15 min	MEDIUM 15-20 min	MEDIUM 12-17 min	MEDIUM 10-15 min

Mullet

See Fish.

Mung Beans

See Pulses.

Mushrooms

Put frozen or fresh (whole or sliced) mushrooms into a casserole, with a knob of butter if wished. Cover and cook until just tender, stirring occasionally.

MUSHROOMS	500W	600-700W	750-850W	900-1000W
115g/4 oz	HIGH 2-3 min	HIGH 1-2 min	MED-HIGH 1-2 min	MED-HIGH 1-2 min
225g/8 oz	HIGH 3-4 min	HIGH 2-3 min	HIGH 1-3 min	MED-HIGH 1-3 min
450g/1 lb	HIGH 6-8 min	HIGH 4-6 min	HIGH 3-5 min	HIGH 3-5 min

Reheating
Put cooked mushrooms into a dish and cover. In all models, simply cook on MED-HIGH until hot throughout, stirring occasionally.

Mussels

See Fish.

Nuts

To 'toast' nuts, spread flaked or chopped nuts in an even layer in a shallow ovenproof dish. Cook, uncovered and stirring frequently, until golden brown. Check them often – they can easily burn.

NUTS	500W	600-700W	750-850W	900-1000W
115g/4 oz	HIGH 5-7 min	HIGH 4-5 min	MED-HIGH 4-5 min	MED-HIGH 4-5 min

Okra

Put sliced or whole small okra into a casserole and add 2-4 tbsp water. Cover and cook until just tender, stirring or shaking occasionally.

OKRA	500W	600-700W	750-850W	900-1000W
115g/4 oz	HIGH 4-5 min	HIGH 3-4 min	MED-HIGH 3-4 min	MED-HIGH 2-3 min
225g/8 oz	HIGH 6-8 min	HIGH 4-6 min	HIGH 3-5 min	MED-HIGH 3-5 min
450g/1 lb	HIGH 9-11 min	HIGH 6-8 min	HIGH 5-7 min	MED-HIGH 5-7 min

Reheating
Put cooked okra into a dish and cover. In all models, simply cook on MEDIUM until hot throughout, stirring occasionally.

Onions

Frozen

Put the frozen onions into a casserole and cover. Cook until just tender, stirring occasionally.

ONIONS	500W	600-700W	750-850W	900-1000W
115g/4 oz	HIGH 3-4 min	HIGH 2-3 min	MED-HIGH 2-3 min	MEDIUM 3-4 min
225g/8 oz	HIGH 5-7 min	HIGH 4-6 min	HIGH 3-5 min	MED-HIGH 3-5 min
450g/1 lb	HIGH 7-10 min	HIGH 6-9 min	HIGH 5-7 min	HIGH 5-7 min

Fresh

Put sliced or whole baby onions into a casserole with 2-4 tbsp water. Cover and cook until just tender, stirring occasionally.

ONIONS	500W	600-700W	750-850W	900-1000W
115g/4 oz	HIGH 4-6 min	HIGH 3-4 min	MED-HIGH 3-4 min	MED-HIGH 2-3 min
225g/8 oz	HIGH 6-9 min	HIGH 5-7 min	HIGH 3-5 min	MED-HIGH 3-5 min
450g/1 lb	HIGH 12-14 min	HIGH 9-11 min	HIGH 8-10 min	HIGH 7-9 min

Reheating

Put the cooked onions into a covered dish, with a knob of butter if wished. In all models, heat on MEDIUM, stirring occasionally, until piping hot.

Oranges and Lemons

To squeeze extra juice from oranges and lemons, warm them in the microwave first.

ORANGES & LEMONS	500W	600-700W	750-850W	900-1000W
1 medium	HIGH 1-1½ min	HIGH 1 min	MED-HIGH 1 min	MED-HIGH 30-45 sec
2 medium	HIGH 2-3 min	HIGH 1-2 min	HIGH 1-1½ min	MED-HIGH 1-1½ min

Parsnips

Frozen
Put the frozen parsnips into a casserole and cover. Cook until just tender, stirring occasionally.

PARSNIPS	500W	600-700W	750-850W	900-1000W
115g/4 oz	HIGH 5-7 min	HIGH 4-5 min	MED-HIGH 3-5 min	MED-HIGH 3-4 min
225g/8 oz	HIGH 9-11 min	HIGH 6-8 min	HIGH 5-7 min	HIGH 4-6 min
450g/1 lb	HIGH 12-15 min	HIGH 9-11 min	HIGH 8-10 min	HIGH 7-9 min

Fresh
Put sliced parsnips into a casserole with 2-4 tbsp water. Cover and cook until just tender, stirring occasionally.

PARSNIPS	500W	600-700W	750-850W	900-1000W
115g/4 oz	HIGH 5-6 min	HIGH 4-5 min	MED-HIGH 4-5 min	MEDIUM 5-6 min
225g/8 oz	HIGH 8-10 min	HIGH 6-8 min	HIGH 5-7 min	MED-HIGH 5-7 min
450g/1 lb	HIGH 10-12 min	HIGH 8-10 min	HIGH 7-9 min	HIGH 6-8 min

Reheating
See Vegetables.

Pasta

Put the pasta into a deep, wide casserole and cover gener-
ously with boiling water (from the kettle). Stir well. Cook,
uncovered, until almost cooked (*al dente*), stirring once or
twice. Cover and leave to stand for 5 minutes, during
which time the pasta will continue softening. Drain well
before serving.

PASTA – dried	500W	600-700W	750-850W	900-1000W
115g/4 oz	HIGH 7-10 min	HIGH 7-9 min	HIGH 7-9 min	MED-HIGH 7-9 min
225g/8 oz	HIGH 8-11 min	HIGH 8-10 min	HIGH 8-10 min	MED-HIGH 8-10 min

PASTA – fresh	500W	600-700W	750-850W	900-1000W
115g/4 oz	HIGH 2-4 min	HIGH 2-3 min	HIGH 2-3 min	MED-HIGH 2-3 min
225g/8 oz	HIGH 3-5 min	HIGH 3-4 min	HIGH 3-4 min	MED-HIGH 3-4 min

Reheating
Put the cooked pasta into a casserole, cover and heat until
piping hot throughout, stirring once or twice. If wished,
add a knob of butter, a little oil or a tablespoon or two of
liquid (water or stock) during heating to keep the pasta
moist and the pieces separate.

PASTA – reheating	500W	600-700W	750-850W	900-1000W
1 serving	HIGH 1-2 min	HIGH 1/2-1 min	MED-HIGH 1/2-1 min	MEDIUM 1-2 min
2 servings	HIGH 2-3 min	HIGH 1-2 min	MED-HIGH 1-2 min	MEDIUM 2-3 min
4 servings	HIGH 3-5 min	HIGH 2-4 min	HIGH 2-3 min	MED-HIGH 3-4 min

Pastry – raw

Thawing

Unwrap the shortcrust or puff pastry and put it on a sheet of kitchen paper. Microwave until it just begins to soften. Leave to stand until completely thawed before using. These times are for purchased packets of frozen pastry.

PASTRY – thawing	500W	600-700W	750-850W	900-1000W
400g/14 oz packet	DEFROST 3 min	DEFROST 2 min	DEFROST 2 min	DEFROST 1 1/2 min

Peaches

Skin, halve and stone the peaches. Put the peach halves into a casserole with 2-4 tbsp water, wine, cider or fruit juice. Cover and cook until just tender, stirring occasionally. Sweeten to taste if necessary.

PEACHES	500W	600-700W	750-850W	900-1000W
115g/4 oz	HIGH 3-4 min	HIGH 2-3 min	MED-HIGH 2-3 min	MEDIUM 3-4 min
225g/8 oz	HIGH 5-7 min	HIGH 4-6 min	HIGH 3-5 min	MED-HIGH 3-5 min
450g/1 lb	HIGH 7-10 min	HIGH 6-9 min	HIGH 5-7 min	HIGH 5-7 min

Pears

Peel, halve and core the pears and cut into slices. Put into a casserole with 2-4 tbsp water, fruit juice, sweet cider or wine (add a cinnamon stick too for a spicy flavour). Cover and cook until soft, stirring gently occasionally. Sweeten to taste if necessary.

PEARS	500W	600-700W	750-850W	900-1000W
115g/4 oz	HIGH 3-4 min	HIGH 2-3 min	MED-HIGH 2-3 min	MEDIUM 3-4 min
225g/8 oz	HIGH 5-7 min	HIGH 4-6 min	HIGH 3-5 min	MED-HIGH 3-5 min
450g/1 lb	HIGH 7-10 min	HIGH 6-9 min	HIGH 5-7 min	HIGH 5-7 min

Peas

Frozen
Tip the frozen peas into a casserole, cover and cook until just tender, stirring occasionally.

PEAS	500W	600-700W	750-850W	900-1000W
115g/4 oz	HIGH 4-5 min	HIGH 3-4 min	MED-HIGH 3-4 min	MED-HIGH 2-3 min
225g/8 oz	HIGH 6-8 min	HIGH 5-6 min	HIGH 4-5 min	MED-HIGH 4-6 min
450g/1 lb	HIGH 8-10 min	HIGH 6-8 min	HIGH 5-7 min	HIGH 5-6 min

Fresh
Put the peas into a casserole with 2-4 tbsp water. Cover and cook until just tender, stirring occasionally.

PEAS	500W	600-700W	750-850W	900-1000W
115g/4 oz	HIGH 4-6 min	HIGH 2-4 min	MED-HIGH 2-4 min	MEDIUM 4-6 min
225g/8 oz	HIGH 4-6 min	HIGH 3-5 min	HIGH 3-5 min	MED-HIGH 3-5 min
450g/1 lb	HIGH 5-9 min	HIGH 4-7 min	HIGH 4-6 min	HIGH 3-6 min

Reheating
Put the cooked peas into a casserole and cover. In all models, simply cook on MEDIUM until hot throughout, stirring occasionally.

Dried
See Pulses.

Pies

Reheating

Reheat cooked pies in the microwave only if you will be happy with less-than-crisp pastry. Remove any foil packaging. Put the pie(s) on a microwave rack and, with a sharp knife, pierce the pastry lids in a few places. Heat until the pastry feels warm (the filling inside will be hotter). Take care not to overheat or the pastry will become soggy and chewy. Leave to stand for a minute or two before serving.

PIES – meat, poultry, fish	500W	600-700W	750-850W	900-1000W
Individual	HIGH 1-2 min	HIGH $1/2$ to $1^1/2$ min	MED-HIGH $1/2$ to $1^1/2$ min	MEDIUM 1-2 min
2 x individual	HIGH $1^1/2$-3 min	HIGH 1-2 min	MED-HIGH 1-2 min	MEDIUM $1^1/2$-3 min
Family-size	HIGH $6^1/2$-9 min	HIGH 5-7 min	MED-HIGH 5-7 min	MED-HIGH 4-$5^1/2$ min

PIES – fruit	500W	600-700W	750-850W	900-1000W
Individual	HIGH 1-$1^1/2$ min	HIGH $1/2$-1 min	MED-HIGH $1/2$-1 min	MEDIUM 1-$1^1/2$ min
2 x individual	HIGH $1^1/2$-2 min	HIGH 1-$1^1/2$ min	MED-HIGH 1-$1^1/2$ min	MEDIUM $1^1/2$-2 min
Family-size	HIGH 2-4 min	MEDIUM 2-4 min	MEDIUM 2-4 min	MEDIUM 2-4 min

Pizza

Pizzas are best cooked conventionally, unless you have a browning dish – in which case, follow the manufacturer's instructions.

Plaice

See Fish.

Plated Meal

A plate of cooked food reheats easily and quickly in the microwave. Arrange the food evenly on the plate, leaving a small area at the centre clear or arranging thinly sliced meat on the centre of the plate. Cover and cook until piping hot throughout. When heating two plates, use a plate ring to separate them and rearrange the plates half way through heating. Leave the plates, covered, to stand for a few minutes before serving.

PLATED MEALS	500W	600-700W	750-850W	900-1000W
1 plate	HIGH 3-4 min	MED-HIGH 3-4 min	MEDIUM 4-5 min	MEDIUM 3-4 min
2 plates	HIGH 4-6 min	MED-HIGH 4-6 min	MEDIUM 5-7 min	MEDIUM 4-6 min

Plums

Halve and stone the plums. Put into a casserole (no need to add extra liquid unless you want to), cover and cook until soft, stirring gently occasionally. Sweeten to taste.

PLUMS	500W	600-700W	750-850W	900-1000W
115g/4 oz	HIGH 3-4 min	HIGH 2-3 min	MED-HIGH 2-3 min	MEDIUM 3-4 min
225g/8 oz	HIGH 5-7 min	HIGH 4-6 min	HIGH 3-5 min	MED-HIGH 3-5 min
450g/1 lb	HIGH 7-9 min	HIGH 6-8 min	HIGH 5-7 min	HIGH 4-6 min

Polenta

Put instant polenta (cornmeal) into a casserole. Season with salt and stir in boiling water (from the kettle) or stock (see chart for quantities) until the mixture is smooth. Cook, uncovered, stirring occasionally, until the polenta thickens and leaves the sides of the casserole. Stir in a generous knob of butter and, if wished, some freshly grated Parmesan cheese and/or some chopped fresh herbs.

POLENTA	500W	600-700W	750-850W	900-1000W
50g/2 oz + 300ml/½ pt boiling liquid (serves 1)	HIGH 6-8 min	HIGH 4-6 min	HIGH 3-5 min	MED-HIGH 3-5 min
115g/4 oz + 600ml/1 pt boiling liquid (serves 2)	HIGH 9-11 min	HIGH 6-8 min	HIGH 5-7 min	MED-HIGH 5-7 min
225g/8 oz + 1.2 litre/2 pt boiling liquid (serves 4)	HIGH 10-12 min	HIGH 8-9 min	HIGH 7-8 min	HIGH 7-8 min

Poppadums

Brush one side of a poppadum with a little oil and cook until crisp and puffed up. It's a good idea, until you know exactly how long it takes in your own microwave, to watch the poppadum cook and remove it as soon as it has puffed up all over. To cook two, just lay one on top of the other.

POPPADUMS	500W	600-700W	750-850W	900-1000W
1	HIGH 1-2 min	HIGH 1 min	HIGH ½-1 min	MED-HIGH ½-1 min
2	HIGH 1½-2 min	HIGH 1-1½ min	HIGH 1 min	MED-HIGH 1 min

Pork

Thawing

Remove any metal ties. Stand the meat on a rack in a shallow dish or put mince into a large bowl. Cover and microwave, turning over (joints) or separating (pieces and mince) occasionally and pouring away any moisture which collects beneath the rack. Take care not to overheat the pork, or some parts may begin cooking while other areas remain frozen. Leave joints to stand at least 30 min before cooking, chops and mince for 10 min.

PORK – thawing	500W	600-700W	750-850W	900-1000W
joints: **per 450g/1 lb**	DEFROST 9-10 min	DEFROST 7-8 min	DEFROST 6-7 min	LOW 7-10 min
chops: **225g/8 oz**	DEFROST 8-9 min	DEFROST 6-7 min	DEFROST 5-6 min	LOW 6-8 min
per 450g/1 lb	DEFROST 10-12 min	DEFROST 8-10 min	DEFROST 7-9 min	LOW 7-9 min
cubes/mince: **115g/4 oz**	DEFROST 4-6 min	DEFROST 3-5 min	DEFROST 3-4 min	LOW 4-6 min
225g/8 oz	DEFROST 6-8 min	DEFROST 5-7 min	DEFROST 4-6 min	LOW 6-8 min
per 450g/1 lb	DEFROST 9-12 min	DEFROST 7-10 min	DEFROST 6-8 min	LOW 7-9 min

Cooking

Joints can be cooked in the microwave but, unless you have a combination microwave cooker (with convected heat as well as microwaves), you may prefer to cook them in the conventional oven. To microwave a joint, put it on a rack in a shallow dish and cover with a split microwave or roasting bag. Turn over occasionally during cooking.

Chops are best cooked on a preheated browning dish – follow the manufacturer's instructions and turn the chops over once during cooking.

PORK	500W	600-700W	750-850W	900-1000W
joints: **per 450g/1 lb**	HIGH 10-13 min	HIGH 8-10 min	MED-HIGH 8-10 min	MEDIUM 10-13 min
chops: 1	HIGH 3-5 min	HIGH 2-4 min	MED-HIGH 2-4 min	MEDIUM 3-5 min
2	HIGH 4-6 min	HIGH 3-5 min	MED-HIGH 3-5 min	MEDIUM 4-6 min
3	HIGH 5-7 min	HIGH 4-6 min	MED-HIGH 4-6 min	MEDIUM 5-7 min
4	HIGH 6-8 min	HIGH 5-7 min	MED-HIGH 5-7 min	MEDIUM 6-8 min

Reheating

A cooked joint of pork is best reheated in slices (and, even better, in gravy). Arrange slices evenly on a plate and cover. In all models, cook on MEDIUM until piping hot throughout.

Porridge

Put the porridge oats in a bowl (large enough to allow the porridge to boil up) and stir in the milk. Cook, uncovered and stirring frequently, until the porridge thickens and boils. Leave to stand for a minute or two, then serve with salt, sugar or honey.

PORRIDGE	500W	600-700W	750-850W	900-1000W
25g/1 oz + 150ml/¼ pt milk	HIGH 3-4 min	HIGH 2-3 min	HIGH 2-3 min	MEDIUM 3-4 min
55g/2 oz + 300ml/½ pt milk	HIGH 4-6 min	HIGH 3-4 min	HIGH 2-3 min	HIGH 2-3 min
100g/3½ oz + 600ml/1 pt milk	HIGH 6-8 min	HIGH 5-7 min	HIGH 4-6 min	HIGH 4-5 min

Potatoes

Cooking

To cook whole jacket potatoes, scrub and dry them, then prick their skins with a fork in several places. Arrange them in a circle in the microwave and cook until tender, turning them over once. Leave to stand for 2-3 minutes before splitting and serving them.

JACKET POTATOES	500W	600-700W	750-850W	900-1000W
1 x 175-225g/ 6-8 oz	HIGH 6-8 min	HIGH 5-6 min	MED-HIGH 5-6 min	MED-HIGH 4-6 min
2 x 175-225g/ 6-8 oz	HIGH 10-12 min	HIGH 8-10 min	MED-HIGH 8-10 min	MED-HIGH 7-9 min
3 x 175-225g/ 6-8 oz	HIGH 12-15 min	HIGH 9-12 min	HIGH 8-10 min	HIGH 7-9 min
4 x 175-225g/ 6-8 oz	HIGH 15-20 min	HIGH 10-15 min	HIGH 9-12 min	HIGH 8-11 min

To cook cut maincrop potatoes or new potatoes, put them into a large casserole with 4 tbsp water. Cover and cook, stirring occasionally, until tender. Leave to stand for a few minutes before serving as they are, or mashing with milk and butter.

CUT OR NEW POTATOES	500W	600-700W	750-850W	900-1000W
225g/8 oz	HIGH 8-9 min	HIGH 6-7 min	MED-HIGH 6-7 min	MED-HIGH 5-6 min
450g/1 lb	HIGH 10-12 min	HIGH 8-10 min	MED-HIGH 8-10 min	MED-HIGH 7-9 min

Reheating

Put cooked jacket potatoes on a plate and pierce their skins in a few places. Heat to serving temperature and leave to stand for 2-3 minutes before serving.

JACKET POTATOES – reheating	500W	600-700W	750-850W	900-1000W
1 x 175-225g/ 6-8 oz	HIGH 2-3 min	HIGH 1-2 min	MED-HIGH 1-2 min	MEDIUM 2-3 min
2 x 175-225g/ 6-8 oz	HIGH 3-4 min	HIGH 2-3 min	MED-HIGH 2-3 min	MED-HIGH 1½ to 2½ min
4 x 175-225g/ 6-8 oz	HIGH 4-6 min	HIGH 3-5 min	HIGH 3-5 min	HIGH 2-4 min

Put mashed potatoes into a dish, cover and microwave, stirring occasionally, until hot throughout.

MASHED POTATOES – reheating	500W	600-700W	750-850W	900-1000W
1 serving	HIGH 40-60 sec	HIGH 30-50 sec	MED-HIGH 30-50 sec	MEDIUM 40-60 sec
2 servings	HIGH 1½-2 min	HIGH 1 min	MED-HIGH 1 min	MEDIUM 1½-2 min
4 servings	HIGH 2-3½ min	HIGH 1½ to 2½ min	MED-HIGH 1½ to 2½ min	MED-HIGH 1½-2 min

Prawns

See Fish.

Pulses

Split peas and lentils do not need soaking before cooking. All other pulses need several hours' (or overnight) soaking in plenty of water before cooking. Alternatively, you can speed things up by pouring over a generous quantity of boiling water (from the kettle), covering and leaving the pulses to stand for 1-2 hours. Drain off and discard the soaking liquid and put the pulses into a deep, wide casserole. Pour over sufficient boiling water to cover them by at least 2.5cm/1 in. Cook, uncovered, stirring occasionally, until tender. Keep your eye on the water level during cooking – if the pulses look as if they might boil dry, top up with extra boiling water (from the kettle). Cover and leave to stand for about 5 minutes before draining and using them.

Remember: some pulses, and red kidney beans in particular, need rapid boiling for 10 minutes in order to destroy toxins. For this reason and because it is sometimes difficult to see when the contents are at a full rolling boil, I find it more convenient to cook on HIGH throughout.

PULSES: 225g/8 oz + boiling water to cover generously	ALL MODELS
Aduki beans	HIGH 30-35 min
Black-eye beans	HIGH 25-35 min
Butter beans	HIGH 30-40 min
Cannellini beans	HIGH 30-45 min
Chick peas	HIGH 50-60 min
Flageolet beans	HIGH 35-45 min

Haricot beans	HIGH 25-35 min
Lentils	HIGH 25-35 min
Mung beans	HIGH 20-30 min
Peas, dried	HIGH 30-45 min
Peas, split	HIGH 25-35 min
Red kidney beans	HIGH 30-45 min

Reheating

Put the cooked beans or peas into a casserole with 2-4 tbsp water or stock. In all models, simply cover and cook on MED-HIGH until hot throughout, stirring occasionally.

Quiche

See Flan – Savoury.

Quinoa

Put the quinoa into a casserole with boiling water or stock (see chart for quantities). Cover and cook, then leave to stand for about 5 minutes before seasoning it, stirring and serving.

QUINOA	500W	600-700W	750-850W	900-1000W
115g/4 oz + 300ml/½ pt boiling liquid	HIGH 12-15 min	HIGH 9-12 min	HIGH 8-10 min	MED-HIGH 8-10 min
225g/8 oz + 600ml/1 pt boiling liquid	HIGH 15-18 min	HIGH 11-14 min	HIGH 10-12 min	MED-HIGH 10-12 min

Raspberries

Thawing
Put the frozen raspberries into a dish, cover and micro-wave on DEFROST, stirring gently occasionally. Leave to stand until completely thawed before using, stirring gently once or twice.

RASPBERRIES – thawing	500W	600-700W	750-850W	900-1000W
115g/4 oz	DEFROST 1½-3 min	DEFROST 1-2 min	DEFROST 1-2 min	DEFROST ½ to 1½ min
225g/8 oz	DEFROST 4-6 min	DEFROST 3-5 min	DEFROST 2½ to 4½ min	DEFROST 2-4 min
450g/1 lb	DEFROST 8-10 min	DEFROST 6-8 min	DEFROST 5-7 min	DEFROST 4-6 min

Cooking
Put frozen or fresh raspberries into a casserole (no need to add extra liquid unless you want to), cover and cook until soft, stirring gently occasionally. (See table overleaf.) Sweeten to taste with sugar or honey.

RASPBERRIES	500W	600-700W	750-850W	900-1000W
115g/4 oz	HIGH 2-4 min	HIGH 1-3 min	MED-HIGH 1-3 min	MEDIUM 2-4 min
225g/8 oz	HIGH 3-5 min	HIGH 2-4 min	MED-HIGH 2-4 min	MED-HIGH 2-3 min
450g/1 lb	HIGH 4-7 min	HIGH 3-6 min	HIGH 3-5 min	HIGH 2-4 min

Red Kidney Beans

See Pulses.

Redcurrants

Thawing

Put the frozen redcurrants into a dish, cover and micro-wave on DEFROST, stirring gently occasionally. Leave to stand until completely thawed before using, stirring gently once or twice.

REDCURRANTS – thawing	500W	600-700W	750-850W	900-1000W
115g/4 oz	DEFROST 1^1/$_2$-3 min	DEFROST 1-2 min	DEFROST 1-2 min	DEFROST ^{1}/$_2$ to 1^1/$_2$ min
225g/8 oz	DEFROST 4-6 min	DEFROST 3-5 min	DEFROST 2^1/$_2$ to 4^1/$_2$ min	DEFROST 2-4 min
450g/1 lb	DEFROST 8-10 min	DEFROST 6-8 min	DEFROST 5-7 min	DEFROST 4-6 min

Cooking

Put frozen or fresh redcurrants into a casserole (no need to add extra liquid unless you want to), cover and cook until soft, stirring gently occasionally. Sweeten to taste with sugar or honey. Leave to stand for a few minutes before using.

REDCURRANTS	500W	600-700W	750-850W	900-1000W
115g/4 oz	HIGH 2-4 min	HIGH 1-3 min	MED-HIGH 1-3 min	MEDIUM 2-4 min
225g/8 oz	HIGH 3-5 min	HIGH 2-4 min	MED-HIGH 2-4 min	MED-HIGH 2-3 min
450g/1 lb	HIGH 4-7 min	HIGH 3-6 min	HIGH 3-5 min	HIGH 2-4 min

Rhubarb

Put frozen or fresh rhubarb into a casserole with sugar to taste (no need to add extra liquid unless you want to, in which case a little fresh orange juice complements the flavour of rhubarb). Cover and cook until just soft, stirring gently occasionally.

RHUBARB	500W	600-700W	750-850W	900-1000W
115g/4 oz	HIGH 2-4 min	HIGH 1-3 min	MED-HIGH 1-3 min	MEDIUM 2-4 min
225g/8 oz	HIGH 3-5 min	HIGH 2-4 min	MED-HIGH 2-4 min	MED-HIGH 2-3 min
450g/1 lb	HIGH 5-8 min	HIGH 4-7 min	HIGH 3-6 min	HIGH 3-5 min

Rice

Put the rice into a deep, wide casserole and stir in boiling water (from the kettle). See charts for quantities. Stir well. Cook, uncovered, until almost all the water has been absorbed. Stir, then cover and leave to stand for 5 minutes (the rice will continue softening and all the water will be absorbed). Fluff the rice up with a fork before serving. To serve the rice cold, or if you plan to reheat it, stir in a tablespoon of oil before leaving it to cool – this will help to keep the grains separate.

RICE – white long grain	500W	600-700W	750-850W	900-1000W
115g/4 oz + 400ml/14 fl oz boiling water	HIGH 10 min	HIGH 10 min	HIGH 10 min	MED-HIGH 10 min
225g/8 oz + 700ml/1¼ pt boiling water	HIGH 10-12 min	HIGH 10-12 min	HIGH 10-11 min	MED-HIGH 10-11 min

RICE – brown	500W	600-700W	750-850W	900-1000W
115g/4 oz + 600ml/1 pt boiling water	HIGH 20-25 min	HIGH 20-25 min	HIGH 20-25 min	MED-HIGH 20-25 min
225g/8 oz + 1 litre/1¾ pt boiling water	HIGH 25-30 min	HIGH 25-30 min	HIGH 25-30 min	MED-HIGH 25-30 min

Reheating

Put the cooked rice into a casserole, cover and heat until piping hot throughout, stirring once or twice. If wished, add a tablespoon or two of liquid (water or stock) during heating to keep the rice moist.

RICE – reheating	500W	600-700W	750-850W	900-1000W
1 serving	HIGH 1-2 min	HIGH 1 min	MED-HIGH 1 min	MEDIUM 1-2 min
2 servings	HIGH 3-4 min	HIGH 2-3 min	MED-HIGH 2-3 min	MED-HIGH 2 min
4 servings	HIGH 5-6 min	HIGH 4-5 min	HIGH 3-4 min	MED-HIGH 3-4 min

Salmon

See Fish.

Sauces

Thawing
Put the sauce into a bowl or jug, cover and microwave, breaking up the sauce with a fork as it thaws.

SAUCE: Meat, Tomato, White – thawing	500W	600-700W	750-850W	900-1000W
300ml/½ pt	DEFROST 10-15 min	DEFROST 8-12 min	DEFROST 7-11 min	DEFROST 6-9 min
600ml/1 pt	DEFROST 16-20 min	DEFROST 12-15 min	DEFROST 10-13 min	DEFROST 9-12 min

Reheating
Pour the sauce into a jug or bowl and cook, stirring occasionally, until piping hot. (See table overleaf.)

MEAT SAUCE e.g. Bolognese	500W	600-700W	750-850W	900-1000W
300ml/½ pt	HIGH 5-7 min	HIGH 4-5 min	MED-HIGH 4-5 min	MED-HIGH 3-4 min
600ml/1 pt	HIGH 10-12 min	HIGH 8-10 min	HIGH 7-9 min	HIGH 6-8 min

TOMATO SAUCE	500W	600-700W	750-850W	900-1000W
300ml/½ pt	HIGH 4-5 min	HIGH 3-4 min	MED-HIGH 3-4 min	MED-HIGH 3-4 min
600ml/1 pt	HIGH 7-9 min	HIGH 5-7 min	HIGH 4-6 min	HIGH 3½ to 5½ min

WHITE SAUCE – sweet or savoury	500W	600-700W	750-850W	900-1000W
300ml/½ pt	HIGH 3-4 min	HIGH 2-3 min	MED-HIGH 2-3 min	MED-HIGH 2-3 min
600ml/1 pt	HIGH 5-7 min	HIGH 4-5 min	HIGH 4-5 min	HIGH 3-4 min

Sausage Rolls

Thawing

Sausage rolls are best left to thaw in the conventional way – to avoid heating the pastry (and therefore making it soggy) before the sausagemeat has thawed.

Reheating

These are fine, so long as you do not expect the pastry to stay crisp. Arrange the sausage rolls on a microwave rack or a preheated browning dish (follow the manufacturer's instructions). Heat until the pastry feels just warm – the sausagemeat filling will be hotter. Leave to stand for a minute or two before serving.

SAUSAGE ROLLS	500W	600-700W	750-850W	900-1000W
2	HIGH 20-30 sec	MED-HIGH 20-30 sec	MEDIUM 30-40 sec	MEDIUM 20-30 sec
4	HIGH 30-50 sec	MED-HIGH 30-50 sec	MEDIUM 40-60 sec	MEDIUM 30-50 sec
6	HIGH 1-1$\frac{1}{2}$ min	MED-HIGH 1-1$\frac{1}{2}$ min	MEDIUM 1$\frac{1}{2}$-2 min	MEDIUM 1-1$\frac{1}{2}$ min

Sausages

These are best cooked conventionally, unless you have a browning dish – in which case, follow the manufacturer's instructions.

Scallops

See Fish.

Shepherd's Pie

Thawing

Remove any foil packaging and put into a close-fitting dish. Cover and microwave. Leave to stand for 10-15 min before reheating.

SHEPHERD'S PIE – thawing	500W	600-700W	750-850W	900-1000W
1 serving	DEFROST 9-11 min	DEFROST 7-8 min	DEFROST 6-7 min	DEFROST 5-6 min
Family-size	DEFROST 13-19 min	DEFROST 10-15 min	DEFROST 8-12 min	DEFROST 7-11 min

Reheating

Remove any foil packaging and put into a close-fitting dish. With a sharp knife, pierce the pie in several places – to help it to heat evenly. Cover and cook until piping hot throughout. Leave to stand for 3-5 min before serving.

SHEPHERD'S PIE	500W	600-700W	750-850W	900-1000W
1 serving	HIGH 3-4 min	MEDIUM 4-6 min	MEDIUM 4-5 min	MEDIUM 3-4 min
Family-size	HIGH 10-15 min	MEDIUM 15-20 min	MEDIUM 12-17 min	MEDIUM 10-15 min

Sole

See Fish.

Soup

Thawing

Put the soup into a bowl, cover and microwave, breaking it up with a fork as it thaws.

SOUP – thawing	500W	600-700W	750-850W	900-1000W
300ml/½ pt	DEFROST 10-15 min	DEFROST 8-12 min	DEFROST 7-11 min	DEFROST 6-9 min
600ml/1 pt	DEFROST 16-20 min	DEFROST 12-15 min	DEFROST 10-13 min	DEFROST 9-12 min

Reheating

Pour the soup into individual bowls, a jug or a casserole. Heat, stirring occasionally, until bubbling hot. Stir again before serving.

SOUP	500W	600-700W	750-850W	900-1000W
1 bowl	HIGH 2-3 min	HIGH 1-2 min	MED-HIGH 1-2 min	MEDIUM 2-3 min
2 bowls	HIGH 3-4 min	HIGH 2-3 min	HIGH 2 min	MED-HIGH 2 min
600ml/1 pt	HIGH 8-10 min	HIGH 6-7 min	HIGH 5-6 min	MED-HIGH 5-6 min

Spaghetti Bolognese

See Sauces.

Spinach

Frozen

Tip frozen leaf or chopped spinach into a casserole, cover and cook until piping hot, separating and stirring occasionally.

SPINACH	500W	600-700W	750-850W	900-1000W
115g/4 oz	HIGH 6-8 min	HIGH 4-6 min	MED-HIGH 3-5 min	MED-HIGH 3-5 min
225g/8 oz	HIGH 8-10 min	HIGH 6-8 min	HIGH 5-7 min	MED-HIGH 5-7 min
450g/1 lb	HIGH 12-14 min	HIGH 9-11 min	HIGH 7-9 min	HIGH 7-9 min

Fresh

Wash and thoroughly drain the spinach, then cut into shreds. Small young leaves can be left whole. Put it, with only the water clinging to its leaves, into a large casserole. Cover and cook until wilted and tender, stirring occasionally. Drain well and stir in butter, seasoning and a pinch of freshly grated nutmeg before serving.

SPINACH	500W	600-700W	750-850W	900-1000W
115g/4 oz	HIGH 3-4 min	HIGH 2-3 min	MED-HIGH 2-3 min	MED-HIGH 2-3 min
225g/8 oz	HIGH 4-5 min	HIGH 3-4 min	HIGH 3-4 min	HIGH 2-3 min
450g/1 lb	HIGH 9-10 min	HIGH 5-6 min	HIGH 4-5 min	HIGH 4-5 min

Reheating

See Vegetables.

Split Peas

See Pulses.

Sponge Pudding

Put 55g/2 oz softened butter or margarine into a bowl and add 55g/2 oz caster sugar, 1 beaten (medium) egg, 115g/4 oz self-raising flour, a drop of vanilla extract and 3 tbsp milk. Beat well until smooth. Spoon the mixture into a lightly-buttered 600ml/1 pt pudding bowl. Cover it loosely with a 'hat' of greaseproof or non-stick paper. Stand the bowl on a microwave rack and cook until well risen – the surface of the pudding should still be slightly moist while the mixture beneath it is cooked. Leave to stand for a few minutes before turning out on to a warmed plate.

SPONGE PUDDING	500W	600-700W	750-850W	900-1000W
As above – to serve 3-4	HIGH 6-8 min	MED-HIGH 6-8 min	MED-HIGH 5-7 min	MEDIUM 6-8 min

Spring Greens

Shred and put into a casserole with 2-4 tbsp water. Cover and cook until just tender, stirring occasionally.

SPRING GREENS	500W	600-700W	750-850W	900-1000W
115g/4 oz	HIGH 4-6 min	HIGH 3-5 min	MED-HIGH 3-5 min	MEDIUM 4-6 min
225g/8oz	HIGH 7-10 min	HIGH 5-7 min	HIGH 4-6 min	MED-HIGH 4-6 min
450g/1 lb	HIGH 9-12 min	HIGH 7-10 min	HIGH 6-8 min	MED-HIGH 6-8 min

Reheating
See Vegetables.

Sprouts

See Brussels Sprouts.

Steak

See Beef.

Swede

Frozen
Tip frozen swede into a casserole, cover and cook until just tender, stirring occasionally.

SWEDE	500W	600-700W	750-850W	900-1000W
115g/4 oz	HIGH 4-5 min	HIGH 3-4 min	MED-HIGH 3-4 min	MED-HIGH 2-3 min
225g/8 oz	HIGH 6-8 min	HIGH 5-6 min	HIGH 4-5 min	HIGH 4-5 min
450g/1 lb	HIGH 8-10 min	HIGH 6-8 min	HIGH 5-7 min	HIGH 5-6 min

Fresh
Put diced swede into a casserole with 2-4 tbsp water. Cover and cook until soft, stirring occasionally.

SWEDE	500W	600-700W	750-850W	900-1000W
115g/4 oz	HIGH 5-7 min	HIGH 4-5 min	MED-HIGH 3-5 min	MED-HIGH 3-4 min
225g/8 oz	HIGH 9-11 min	HIGH 6-8 min	HIGH 5-7 min	HIGH 4-6 min
450g/1 lb	HIGH 12-15 min	HIGH 9-11 min	HIGH 8-10 min	HIGH 7-9 min

Reheating
See Vegetables.

Sweetcorn

Frozen
Tip frozen sweetcorn into a casserole, cover and cook until just tender, stirring occasionally.

SWEETCORN	500W	600-700W	750-850W	900-1000W
115g/4 oz	HIGH 4-6 min	HIGH 3-5 min	MED-HIGH 3-5 min	MED-HIGH 3-5 min
225g/8 oz	HIGH 6-8 min	HIGH 4-6 min	HIGH 3-5 min	MED-HIGH 3-5 min
450g/1 lb	HIGH 9-11 min	HIGH 6-8 min	HIGH 5-7 min	HIGH 5-6 min

Reheating
Put the cooked sweetcorn into a covered dish. In all models, heat on MEDIUM, stirring occasionally, until piping hot.

See also Corn on the Cob.

Tea

Making tea in the microwave is convenient only if you are making one or two cups. Pour cold water into a cup(s) or mug(s) – about 200ml/7 fl oz in each – and heat, stirring once or twice, until it just begins to bubble. Stir the water well, then add a tea bag to each mug. Leave to stand, removing the tea bags when the tea is the required strength. Serve with milk or lemon.

TEA	500W	600-700W	750-850W	900-1000W
1 x 200ml/ 7 fl oz	HIGH 2-3 min	HIGH 1½-2 min	MED-HIGH 1½-2 min	MED-HIGH 1-1½ min
2 x 200ml/7 fl oz	HIGH 3-4 min	HIGH 2-3 min	MED-HIGH 2-3 min	MED-HIGH 2-3 min

Tomatoes

Cut large tomatoes in half and arrange the halves on a plate. Cook them just as they are, or with a small knob of butter and a pinch of sugar on top of each. Cook until just bubbling. Leave to stand for a minute or two before serving, perhaps on hot buttered toast.

TOMATOES	500W	600-700W	750-850W	900-1000W
1 large	HIGH 1½-2 min	HIGH 1-1½ min	MED-HIGH 1-1½ min	MEDIUM 1½-2 min
2 large	HIGH 2-3 min	HIGH 1½ to 2½ min	MED-HIGH 1½ to 2½ min	MEDIUM 2-3 min

Trout

See Fish.

Turkey

Thawing

Remove any metal ties. Stand the turkey on a rack in a shallow dish. Cover and microwave, turning over (whole birds) or separating (portions) occasionally and pouring away any moisture which collects beneath the rack. Leave whole birds to stand at least 30 min before cooking, and portions for at least 10 min.

TURKEY – thawing	500W	600-700W	750-850W	900-1000W
whole: **per 450g/1 lb**	DEFROST 13-15 min	DEFROST 10-12 min	DEFROST 8-10 min	LOW 13-15 min
portions: **225g/8 oz**	DEFROST 4-6 min	DEFROST 3-5 min	DEFROST 3-4 min	LOW 4-6 min
per 450g/1 lb	DEFROST 6-8 min	DEFROST 5-7 min	DEFROST 4-6 min	LOW 6-8 min
cubes/mince: **115g/4 oz**	DEFROST 4-6 min	DEFROST 3-5 min	DEFROST 3-4 min	LOW 4-6 min
225g/8 oz	DEFROST 6-8 min	DEFROST 5-7 min	DEFROST 4-6 min	LOW 6-8 min
per 450g/1 lb	DEFROST 9-12 min	DEFROST 7-10 min	DEFROST 6-8 min	LOW 9-12 min

Cooking

A whole bird can be cooked in the microwave but, unless you have a combination microwave cooker (with convected heat as well as microwaves), you may prefer to cook one in the conventional oven. To microwave a whole turkey, put it on a rack in a shallow dish and cover with a split microwave or roasting bag. Turn over occasionally during cooking.

Portions – arrange in a shallow dish and add a tablespoon or two of stock, wine, fruit juice or water. Cover and cook.

TURKEY	500W	600-700W	750-850W	900-1000W
whole: **per 450g/1 lb**	HIGH 12-14 min	HIGH 9-11 min	MED-HIGH 9-11 min	MEDIUM 12-14 min
portions – with bone: **225g/8 oz**	HIGH 5-7 min	HIGH 4-6 min	MED-HIGH 4-6 min	MEDIUM 5-7 min
per 450g/1 lb	HIGH 8-10 min	HIGH 6-8 min	MED-HIGH 6-8 min	MEDIUM 8-10 min
boneless breast: **225g/8 oz**	HIGH 4-6 min	HIGH 3-5 min	MED-HIGH 3-5 min	MEDIUM 4-6 min
per 450g/1 lb	HIGH 6-8 min	HIGH 5-7 min	MED-HIGH 5-7 min	MEDIUM 6-8 min

Reheating

Cooked turkey is best reheated in pieces (and, preferably, in a sauce). Arrange pieces evenly in a dish and cover. In all models heat on MEDIUM until piping hot throughout.

Turnips

Frozen

Tip frozen turnips into a casserole, cover and cook until just tender, stirring occasionally.

TURNIPS	500W	600-700W	750-850W	900-1000W
115g/4 oz	HIGH 4-5 min	HIGH 3-4 min	MED-HIGH 3-4 min	MED-HIGH 2-3 min
225g/8 oz	HIGH 6-8 min	HIGH 5-6 min	HIGH 4-5 min	HIGH 4-5 min
450g/1 lb	HIGH 8-10 min	HIGH 6-8 min	HIGH 5-7 min	HIGH 5-6 min

Fresh

Put diced turnips into a casserole with 2-4 tbsp water. Cover and cook until just tender, stirring occasionally.

TURNIPS	500W	600-700W	750-850W	900-1000W
115g/4 oz	HIGH 6-7 min	HIGH 4-5 min	MED-HIGH 4-5 min	MED-HIGH 3-5 min
225g/8 oz	HIGH 8-11 min	HIGH 6-8 min	HIGH 5-7 min	HIGH 5-7 min
450g/1 lb	HIGH 12-15 min	HIGH 9-11 min	HIGH 8-10 min	HIGH 7-9 min

Reheating
See Vegetables.

Veal

See Beef.

Vegetables

For cooking times, see individual entries.

See also Blanching Vegetables.

Reheating

Put the cooked vegetables into a dish and cover. Cook, stirring once or twice during heating and again before serving. To serve, add a knob of butter if wished.

VEGETABLES – leafy (cabbage, spinach, spring greens etc)	500W	600-700W	750-850W	900-1000W
1 serving	HIGH 30-40 sec	HIGH 20-30 sec	MED-HIGH 20-30 sec	MEDIUM 30-40 sec
2 servings	HIGH 1 min	HIGH 40-50 sec	MED-HIGH 40-50 sec	MEDIUM 1 min
4 servings	HIGH 1½ to 2½ min	HIGH 1-1½ min	MED-HIGH 1-1½ min	MEDIUM 1½ to 2½ min

VEGETABLES – root (carrots, parsnips, swede, turnips etc)	500W	600-700W	750-850W	900-1000W
1 serving	HIGH 1 min	HIGH 40-50 sec	MED-HIGH 40-50 sec	MEDIUM 1 min
2 servings	HIGH 1½-2 min	HIGH 1-1½ min	MED-HIGH 1-1½ min	MEDIUM 1½-2 min
4 servings	HIGH 3-4 min	HIGH 2-3 min	MED-HIGH 2-3 min	MEDIUM 3-4 min

Three Ways to order *Right Way* books:

1. Visit www.constablerobinson.com and order through our website.
2. Telephone the TBS order line on 01206 255 800.
   Order lines are open Monday – Friday, 8:30am–5:30pm.
3. Use this order form and send a cheque made payable to TBS Ltd or
   charge my ☐ Visa ☐ Mastercard ☐ Maestro (issue no. _____)

Card number: _____

Expiry date: _____ Last three digits on back of card:_____

Signature: _____

(your signature is essential when paying by credit or debit card)

No. of copies	Title	Price	Total
	Microwave Cooking Properly Explained	£5.99	
	Microwave Recipes for One	£4.99	
	The Combination Microwave Cook	£5.99	
	For P&P add £2.75 for the first book, 60p for each additional book		
	Grand Total		£

Name: _____

Address:_____

_____ Postcode: _____

Daytime Tel. No./Email _____
(in case of query)

**Please return forms to Cash Sales/Direct Mail Dept.,
The Book Service, Colchester Road, Frating Green,
Colchester CO7 7DW.**

Enquiries to readers@constablerobinson.com.

Constable and Robinson Ltd (directly or via its agents)
may mail, email or phone you about promotions or products.

☐ Tick box if you do not want these from us ☐ or our subsidiaries.

www.constablerobinson.com